WoRDS GoNE WILD

WORDS GONE WILD

FUN AND GAMES FOR LANGUAGE LOVERS

JIM BERNHARD

SKYHORSE PUBLISHING

Designed by LeAnna Wetter Smith

Skyhorse Publishing books may be purchased in bulk at special discounts for sales promotion, corporate gifts, fund-raising, or educational purposes. Special editions can also be created to specifications. For details, contact the Special Sales Department, Skyhorse Publishing, 555 Eighth Avenue, Suite 903, New York, NY 10018 or info@skyhorsepublishing.com.

www.skyhorsepublishing.com

10 9 8 7 6 5 4 3 2

Library of Congress Cataloging-in-Publication Data

Bernhard, Jim.
  Words gone wild : fun and games for language lovers / by Jim Bernhard.
    p. cm.
  Includes index.
  ISBN 978-1-61608-014-3 (alk. paper)
  1. English language--Humor. I. Title.
  PN6231.W64B45 2010
  827.008--dc22

                                        2010003329

Printed in China

Dialogue from *A Night at the Opera*, screenplay by George S. Kaufman and Morrie Ryskind, produced by Metro-Goldwyn-Mayer, 1935. Used by permission of Warner Bros. Entertainment Inc. • Excerpt from *Gravity's Rainbow*, by Thomas Pynchon, The Viking Press, 1973; Penguin Books editions, 1995, 2000. • Lines from *A Void* by Georges Perec, translated from the French by Gilbert Adair, reprinted by permission of David R. Godine, Publisher, Inc. Copyright © 1969 by Éditions Denoël, Translation copyright © HarperCollins Publishers 1994. • "Washington Crossing the Delaware," by David Shulman and others, from *The Enigma*, June 1936, and December, 1980. Reprinted by permission of National Puzzlers' League, publisher of *The Enigma*. • "Dopamine, Epinephrine, Valentine" and "So many poems I have read," by Paul Bernhard. Used by permission of Paul Bernhard. • "Chacun Gille (11)," from *Mots d'Heures: Gousses Rames* by Luis d'Antin Van Rooten, copyright © 1967 by Courtlandt H. K. Van Rooten. Used by permission of Viking Penguin, a division of Penguin Groups (USA) Inc. • Excerpt from "If I Can't Sell It, I'll Keep Sitting On It," by Andy Razaf and Alexander Hill, copyright 1935. Used by permission of Joe Davis Music, Ellen Davis Morris, 9150 Marlin Drive, Boerne, TX 78006.

For

Ginger

CONTENTS

PREFACE

Easy writing's curst hard reading.

—Richard Brinsley Sheridan, *Clio's Protest*

The title of this book—*Words Gone Wild*—is not entirely fair to the hardworking words between its covers, striving mightily to entertain you. In fact, the words in this cast of characters do their jobs often under more constraints than their lazier cousins who work in serious prose. A word in a pun or a poem or a puzzle has no understudy; no convenient synonym stands by to replace the *mot juste* in a well-turned epigram; there are no do-overs for words that must be precise if they are to do their job properly.

Oh, occasionally you'll find some words in this book that have slipped into careless behavior—those in the malapropisms and spoonerisms, for example. And there are also a few—the ones you'll find in the limericks and double entendres, especially—whose naughty conduct may be justly chastised by some readers. But by and large these "words gone wild" are the most disciplined you will ever come across. Their "wildness" is of the same sort that inspires the split-second reactions of a crackerjack cast in a rip-roaring farce or that propels a slapstick comedian taking a pie in the face. The timing is everything, and there is no room for error. The word "wild" in the title refers to the spirit that motivates these verbal performers: a propensity for mischief, surprise, and laughter. Their wildness is a freeing of the syntactical bonds that hold back other, more staid words and make them boring. The words in this book just want you to have fun. And creating fun is very hard work.

1

This book is certainly not the first foray ever ventured into the quirky world of words, and I am sure it will not be the last. Having fun with words has an eternal fascination, and I am grateful to such pioneers in wordplay as Homer (not Simpson—the Greek one), Aristophanes, the Apostle Matthew, Chaucer, Shakespeare, Sir John Davies, John Dryden, Dr. Samuel Johnson, Richard Brinsley Sheridan, Joseph Addison, Sean O'Tuama, Andrias MacCriath, Benjamin Franklin, Queen Victoria, Lewis Carroll, Edward Lear, Charles Dickens, Edgar Allan Poe, Oscar Wilde, W. S. Gilbert, Mark Twain, Hilaire Belloc, G. K. Chesterton, Oliver Wendell Holmes Sr., Dr. William Archibald Spooner, Edmund Clerihew Bentley, Eugene Field, Ernest Vincent Wright, Georges Perec, T. S. Eliot, W. H. Auden, Ogden Nash, Roy Bongartz, David Shulman, Dmitri A. Borgmann, Howard Bergerson, Jeff Grant, Leigh Mercer, Gelett Burgess, Richard Armour, Morris Bishop, Luis d'Antin van Rooten, Noël Coward, Cole Porter, Lorenz Hart, Ira Gershwin, Andy Razaf, Bertrand Russell, Robert Benchley, Dorothy Parker, H. L. Mencken, W. C. Fields, George S. Kaufman, Morrie Ryskind, Oscar Levant, Bennett Cerf, James Thurber, Louis Untermeyer, Ben Gross, Groucho Marx, Yogi Berra, David Crystal, William S. Baring-Gould, Gershon Legman, Arthur Wynne, Eugene T. Maleska, William Safire, Edwin Newman, Trude Michel Jaffe, Richard Maltby Jr., Stephen Sondheim, Elizabeth Kingsley, Will Shortz, Thomas H. Middleton, Emily Cox, Henry Rathvon, Bill Morgan, Alistair Ferguson Ritchie, Edward Powys Mathers, Derrick Somerset Macnutt, Adrian Bell, Tom Lehrer, Judith Viorst, Ken Parkin, William Poundstone, Reginald Bretnor, Thomas Pynchon, Willard R. Espy, Ross Eckler, Russell Baker, Sylvia Wright, John Mella, Jon Carroll, and many others whom I have shamefully overlooked. They know who they are. Many of them are quoted or referred to in the text of this book, and all of them have amused, instructed, or inspired me.

For definitions, etymologies, and historical facts, I have relied on *Webster's New International Dictionary of the English Language*, second edition (1949); *Merriam-Webster's Collegiate Dictionary*, eleventh edition (2007); *The Compact Edition of the Oxford English Dictionary* (1971); *The Columbia Encyclopedia*, sixth edition (2000); and the indispensable Wikipedia.com. All material quoted from other sources and not otherwise credited is believed either to be in the public domain or to constitute fair use.

Others who provided, often unwittingly, fodder for these pages include my mother, Willye G. Bernhard, and my friends Stephen Baker, Paula Eisenstein Baker, John Russell Brown, James Brannon, Richard Carlson, Christopher Combest, Betty Connors, Carol Conway, Carl Cunningham, A. J. del Rosario, Frank Lloyd Dent, Terrence Doody, Betty Ewing, Bob Feingold, Ange Finn, Michael Freeman, Sandy Graf, Dorothy Hackney, Roy Hamlin, Neil (Sandy) Havens, Helen Morris Havens, D. J. Hobdy, Ann Hitchcock Holmes, Charles Krohn, Charles E. Kuba, Ralph Liese, Anne Marsh, Thad N. Marsh, Patricia Cunningham Marsh, Donna Martin, Toby Mattox, Ava Jean Mears, K. Lype Odell, John E. Parish, Carter Rochelle, Kathryn Rodwell, Charles Rosekrans, Isadore (Izzy) Schmaltzoff, Steve Shepley, Megan Smith, Paul C. Thomas, Harrison Wagner, Ralph Wilton, Susie Works, Frank Young, and several others whose names, like so much else these days, escape me.

My agent, the indefatigable Julia Lord, has been my sine qua non. Her ready wit, vast knowledge, fierce tenacity, and unvarying cheerfulness have earned her a place of honor in these acknowledgments. Ann Treistman, senior editor at Skyhorse Publishing, has been a joy to work with, and her expertise has helped craft the finished volume in innumerable ways.

On a more personal level, my wife, Virginia Bernhard, a brilliant historian and author, has been a keen-eared critic and adviser and, as always, my chief inspiration. My gratitude goes to our children, Catherine, Paul, and Anne, who more-or-less good-naturedly spent much of their childhood subjected to their father's puns, poems, and puzzles, not to mention plenty of palaver and poppycock. In adulthood, all of them have contributed puns and word games to the seething cauldron from which this book erupted. Paul, in fact, is represented in this volume by two examples of his own poetic prowess.

And now, in the sportive spirit of Mardi Gras, or any other festival that may tickle your fancy, *laissez les bons mots rouler!*

WoRDS
GoNE WILD

CHAPTER ONE

ONCE A PUN A TIME

Puns: Homographs, Homophones, Assonants, and Feghoots

"That's a great deal to make one word mean,"
Alice said in a thoughtful tone.
"When I make a word do a lot of work like that,"
said Humpty Dumpty, "I always pay it extra."
—Lewis Carroll, *Through the Looking Glass*

Puns are the potato chips of literature. There's not much substance to them, but they are a ubiquitous garnish, adding zest to more solid fare. What does it matter if sometimes they are a little salty or maybe even downright cheesy? Serious writers from Homer to Thomas Pynchon have dished up puns to add spice to their weighty texts. Readers eat them up, even if they feel a smidgen of guilt in doing so. Face it, whenever we encounter puns (or potato chips), we can't resist the temptation to savor them—even though we scold ourselves for having succumbed to their subversive delectability. Unlike potato chips, puns never go stale. Even if you have already come across some of the puns in this chapter, you can relish them again—and, as you will find, not all puns are potato chips: some are pure corn.

—•◆•—

Two peanuts went into a bar. One was a salted.

—•◆•—

The word *pun* is believed, at least by some etymologists, to be a contraction of the English word *pundigrion* or, possibly, *punnet*— both of which are thankfully now archaic, but in their prime were used to mean a "quibble," a "cavil," or a "small or fine point of argument." Both words derive from the Italian *puntiglio*, which in turn came from the Latin *punctum*, meaning "a small detail." *Pun* was first used as a word in the English Restoration period, sometime in the 1660s. This fascinating etymological history comes from the *Oxford English Dictionary*, which reluctantly admits at the conclusion of its scholarly note that it is all purely conjectural and may not have happened that way at all.

Defining a pun is more clear-cut. According to the *Oxford Companion to the English Language*, a pun is "the conflation of homonyms and near homonyms to produce a humorous effect." No equivocal waffling there!

These Oxford references might lead you to believe that graduates of that esteemed university have a special fondness for this form of humor—all that pun-ting on the Isis, perhaps. But it was an Oxford man, Samuel Johnson, who insisted, "The pun is the lowest form of humor." Johnson, to be sure, was not a true Oxonian, since he had to leave the university after his first year owing to a shortage of funds. Like others who have initially sneered at the pun, however, Dr. Johnson (Oxford finally grudgingly awarded him a degree when he was forty-six) was not above dabbling on occasion in the slums of rhetoric. One of his alleged witticisms concerned two women yelling at each other across an alleyway from their respective houses.

"They'll never agree," Johnson reputedly said, "for they are arguing from different premises."

He seems to have regretted such lapses, although not with true repentance, for he also wrote: "If I were punished for every pun I shed, there would not be left a puny shed of my punnish head."

A latter-day pundit (well, yes, a pun is intended), Oscar Levant, with no known Oxford connections, improved upon Johnson's puntification when he said, "The pun is the lowest form of humor—if you don't think of it first." (It was also Levant—pianist, actor, talk show denizen—who reminded us: "There is a fine line between genius and insanity; I have erased that line.")

—◆—

A man with sleep problems complained to his doctor: "Some nights I dream I'm a tepee, and other nights I dream I'm a wigwam." The doctor told him: "Take it easy—you're two tents."

—◆—

Most puns—maybe all of them if you want to get seriously analytical about it—are one of three types, or a combination of them. A homographic pun uses two or more words that are spelled exactly alike but have different meanings: Why does a match box? Because it sees a tin can.

A homophonic pun exploits words that sound alike, but have different spellings and meanings: The pony was unable to talk because he was a little hoarse.

An assonant pun alludes to one or more words that have a similarity in sound but which are not identical in sound, spelling, or meaning: A woman received a bouquet made up only of ferns and other greenery with no flowers. She said, "With fronds like these, who needs anemones?"

———•———

Actor/tippler John Barrymore was in a speakeasy one evening during Prohibition when it was raided by the police. "We're only going to arrest habitués," said the officer. "That's all right then," said Barrymore, "there's no one here tonight but sons of habitués."

———•———

The poor, put-upon pun seems always to attract crotchety words. Oliver Wendell Holmes, Sr., poet and physician, wrote in *The Autocrat of the Breakfast-Table*: "People who make puns are like wanton boys that put coppers on the railroad tracks. They amuse themselves and other children, but their little trick may upset a freight train of conversation for the sake of a battered witticism. . . . A pun does not commonly justify a blow in return. But if a blow were given for such cause, and death ensued, the jury would be judges both of the facts and of the pun, and might, if the latter were of an aggravated character, return a verdict of justifiable homicide." Mind you, this is the very same Holmes who as a physician assured his patients that he was "grateful for small fevers."

Speaking of Holmes, in this case Sherlock, Sir Arthur Conan Doyle's brother-in-law, E. W. Hornung, once remarked of the famously arrogant fictional detective: "Though he might be more humble, there's no police like Holmes."

In a kind of backhanded compliment, Edgar Allan Poe, in one of his less eerie moments, proclaimed, "The goodness of the true pun is in the direct ratio of its intolerability." He perhaps demonstrated his own capacity to plumb the depths of punniness with his invention of the Dutch borough of Vondervotteimittiss in "The Devil in the Belfry." Of course Poe cannot be held personally responsible for the Baltimore dining establishment called "The Tell-Tale Hearth," which offers "pizza worth raven about" or for the city's "Poe-boy sandwiches."

A stand-up comedian included ten puns in his routine,
hoping at least one would crack up his audience.
Unfortunately, no pun in ten did.

Despite the verbal punishment it has uncomplainingly endured—who among us has not groaned at an egregious one?—the pun boasts a noble literary heritage. You can find puns (if you look hard enough) in the writings of ancient Greeks, including Homer, Sophocles, and, of course, that old funster, Aristophanes. Discerning a pun in translation is always tricky, especially for those of us with small Latin and less Greek, but learned scholars give us such passages from Homer's *Odyssey* as this one in which Odysseus tells his captor, Polyphemus the Cyclops, that his name is "Nobody." Having got Polyphemus drunk on wine, Odysseus blinds him in his one good eye, and when Polyphemus cries for help from his fellow Cyclopses, they call to him, "What's the matter?" Polyphemus replies: "Nobody is trying to kill me. Nobody's treachery is doing me to death." "Well, then," the other Cyclopses all say, "if nobody's harming you, there's nothing we need to do about it." Odysseus and his men then have a good chortle before escaping the blinded Polyphemus by concealing themselves under his sheep as they amble into the pastures.

Greek drama, too, had its share of puns, as in this exchange in Aristophanes' *The Clouds*, a satire on Socratic philosophy, in which

11

Strepsiades inquires about some of the students in Socrates's academy: "Why do those over there stoop down so much?" "Oh, they're diving deep into the deepest secrets." "And why are their rumps turned up to the sky?" "They're taking . . . private lessons on the stars."

The plays on the words "diving deep" in connection with stooping and with learning secrets, and of "private" in connection with rump and with lessons, are unmistakable examples of Aristophanes's irreverent and often bawdy jests.

A butcher backed into his meat-grinder
and got behind in his orders.

On a more serious note—yes, puns can be serious—one of the central symbols of Sophocles's tragedy *Oedipus Rex* is drawn from a pun in Greek mythology, the famed Riddle of the Sphinx. The Sphinx, a monster with a lion's body and a human head, asked travelers to solve this riddle: "What walks on four legs in the morning, two legs at noon, and three legs at night—and the more legs it has the weaker it is?" Oedipus was the only one who knew the answer: "A man crawls on all fours as a baby, walks upright as an adult, and uses a staff to support him when he's old." Although it is not spelled out in the text of the play, the riddle is alluded to and represents the fate not only of Oedipus himself but also of all mankind.

An important Christian tenet is expressed in the Bible with a pun uttered by no less than Jesus Christ. In chapter 16, verse 18, of the Book of Matthew, Jesus tells one of his disciples: "Thou art Peter, and upon this rock I will build my church."

This is a pun that works in many languages, although, alas, not in English. When Jesus recruited Simon as an apostle, he renamed him *Cephas*, which is the Aramaic word for "rock." It makes its way into St. Matthew's Greek as the name *Petros*, which is close enough to *petra*, the Greek for "rock," that the pun still works. Thence into Latin, where Greek has been appropriated for *Petrus* the name and *petra* the rock.

When the passage reaches a French translation, the pun becomes exact once more, as it originally was in Aramaic: "Tu es Pierre, et sur cette pierre je bâtirai mon Église." Even in Spanish and Italian the names for Peter (*Pedro* and *Pietro*) and the words for rock (*piedra* and *pietra*) are still close enough to make the pun's point. But when you get to English, a more literal translation might be "Thou art *Rock*, and upon this rock I will build my church," but the name Rock probably would not have occurred to seventeenth-century English translators as readily as it did to the Hollywood publicist who re-christened Roy Harold Fitzgerald as Rock Hudson. In any event, it would be difficult to use the name in a liturgical setting today, at least with a straight face.

"One man's Mede is another man's Persian."
—George S. Kaufman

By the time Chaucer comes along with his Middle English in the fourteenth century, puns—even though the word itself is not yet known—are more frequent, more comical, and more easily identified by modern readers. In *The Canterbury Tales*, the Pardoner observes:

> "I rekke nevere, whan that they been beryed,
> Though that hir soules goon a-blakeberyed!"

By this he means, as if you didn't know, that he doesn't care what happens to his parishioners' souls after they are *buried*—they can go gather black*berries* for all he cares. And Chaucer didn't even own a BlackBerry! Even without a smartphone, you should have no trouble with the Summoner's invective against a wicked friar, as he prays for his fellow pilgrims: "God save yow alle, save this cursed Frere!" The two meanings of *save* should warrant at least a small chuckle from all but the most monkish.

—•—

A policeman who enjoys reading The Canterbury Tales
is known as a cop and Chaucer.

—•—

The frequency of Shakespeare's punning puts poor old Chaucer to shame. The Bard of Avon punned frequently, blatantly, bawdily, comically, and with impunity.

"Now is the winter of our discontent / Made glorious summer by this sun of York" are the opening lines of *Richard III*, in which Richard refers to the defeat of the Lancastrians by his brother, King Edward, who was the son of the former Duke of York. As Shakespeare's audience would know, the "sun of York" also referred to the appearance in the sky, during the crucial battle, of an optical illusion in which it appeared that there were three suns, a symbol of victory, representing the Father, the Son, and the Holy Ghost. It would be delightful to stretch the pun even further by suggesting that Richard was commenting on the fair weather he was enjoying in York—but, unfortunately, according to Shakespeare he spoke the lines in London, where, of course, the sun never shines.

A few more examples will establish Shakespeare's unshake-able reputation as a long-distance punner. In *Henry IV Part 1*,

Falstaff observes to Hal that it is "here apparent that thou art heir apparent." In *Henry VI Part 2* York expresses his impatience with the Duke of Suffolk thus: "For Suffolk's duke, may he be suffocate." In *Romeo and Juliet*, when Mercutio is mortally wounded by Tybalt, he says: "Ask for me tomorrow, and you shall find me a grave man." In *Henry V*, Pistol vows: "To England will I steal, and there I'll steal."

Enough, Will, enough! Shakespeare was also the master of the naughty pun sometimes known as a double entendre. But you will have to earn your titillation with these additional ribaldries by slogging through several more chapters.

Pistol's line about *stealing to* and *stealing in* England is a type of homographic pun known as an *antanaclasis* (pronounced, says Webster, with the accent on the "nac"). It means using the same word twice, but in two different senses. Some of the better antanaclases that you've probably already heard are:

* "If we do not all hang together, we shall all hang separately." (Benjamin Franklin)
* "If you're not fired with enthusiasm, you'll be fired with enthusiasm." (Vince Lombardi)
* "Put out the light, and then put out the light." (Shakespeare—him again!—*Othello*)
* "I'm seeing spots before my eyes." "Have you seen a doctor?" "No, just spots."

There are also implied antanaclases, in which the punned word does not appear twice, but its two meanings are obviously implied from the context:

* Have your eyes ever been checked? No, they've always been brown.
* Do you file your nails? No, I just throw them away after I've cut them.

A double antanaclasis is also possible, as in "Time flies like an arrow. Fruit flies like a banana," attributed to Groucho Marx. Both the words "flies" and "like" are used in different senses.

"A girl's best friend is her mutter."
—Dorothy Parker

In their films, Groucho and his Marxist brothers never let a word go un-pun-ished if they could help it. Some of their efforts were sublimely elegant—perhaps with the help of George S. Kaufman and Morrie Ryskind, who are credited with many of the screenplays, including this exchange from *A Night at the Opera:*

> Driftwood (Groucho, examining a contract): "Oh, that? Oh, that's the usual clause. That's in every contract. That just says . . . it says . . . 'If any of the parties participating in this contract is shown not to be in their right mind, the entire agreement is automatically nullified.'"
> Fiorello (Chico): "Well, I don't know . . ."
> Driftwood: "It's all right, that's, that's in every contract. That's, that's what they call a 'sanity clause.'"
> Fiorello: "Ha ha ha ha ha! You can't fool me! There ain't no Sanity Clause!"

Here, a combination of assonant words (*Santa* and *sanity*) and homophonic words (*Claus* and *clause*) is the culmination of a neatly structured setup that provides a flawless payoff.

―•―

When Neil Kinnock was the Leader of the British Labour Party, he was leaving the House of Commons just as a group of American tourists approached. The Speaker of the House, still attired in the ceremonial robes of office, hailed Kinnock from several yards away. "Neil!" he called. Dutifully, and with great reverence, the Americans all got down on their knees.

―•―

Among modern works, James Joyce's *Ulysses* and the impenetrable *Finnegans Wake* win the Pullet Surprise for most puns per line of type—more often than not either obscene or so obscure as to be incomprehensible. Among the better ones that fall into neither category is the line in *Ulysses* when Leopold Bloom contemplates his lunch, eyes the items on a shelf in a pub, and then invokes Genesis: "Sandwich? Ham and his descendants mustered and bred there."

The inveterate punster's idea of bliss is to construct an elaborate tale that results in multiple puns. Sometimes they're called shaggy-dog stories. The nineteenth-century U.S. Senator from Illinois Charles B. Farwell, described by the *New York Times* as an "earnest, active Republican" and also as "one of the heartiest of men and most cheery of the well-known prominent citizens of Chicago," had extensive cattle holdings in Texas. He claimed that the only perfect triple pun in the English language concerned the three brothers who inherited three parcels of land from their father and wanted to combine them into one cattle ranch. They didn't know what to name their ranch until their widowed mother suggested: "Focus—for it's where the sons raise meat." A Rice University physics student went Farwell one better than by turning it into a quadruple pun: where the mourning sons raise meat.

The chicken that crossed the road
was pure poultry in motion.

There exists, believe it or not, a kind of pun known as a "feghoot." Similar to a shaggy-dog story, it can be defined as an elaborate vignette, the conclusion of which is a lengthy pun so atrocious as to guarantee gapes of disbelief from the listeners who have stayed long enough to hear it out. The origin of this kind of pun was a series of science fiction stories that appeared under the collective title "Through Time and Space with Ferdinand Feghoot" by Grendel Briarton, which is an anagram (q.v.) of the real Reginald Bretnor. Initially published in *Fantasy and Science Fiction* magazine between 1956 and 1973, the stories' usual formula was for the title character to resolve an elaborately complicated situation by invoking an absurdly contrived pun, based on a well-known phrase and usually involving a spoonerism (q.v.).

One such tale, in the magazine's July 1961 issue, had Feghoot arriving on a planet whose inhabitants were all small pearls (aw, c'mon, it's sci-fi). Long story short: the Pearly Queen was distraught because her lawyer, Michael, had decided to commit suicide, owing to his unhappiness that his outer surface was pitted and pockmarked, not smooth like other pearls. His fatal method would be to amble along

18

the seashore until the repeated action of the incoming tides dissolved him (this might take a while, as you can see). Feghoot agreed to try to rescue him and soon succeeded. When asked how he did it, he replied (pay attention now) that he simply walked barefoot on the beach until he felt something rough between his toes, because, as the song lyric says, "A gritty pearl is Michael, L.L.D." (You may have to read that last phrase aloud, and you may then be sorry that you did.)

Thomas Pynchon, in his 1973 novel *Gravity's Rainbow*, creates a convoluted setup for a feghoot in the character of Chiclitz, who deals in furs, which are delivered to his storehouse by a group of youngsters. Chiclitz confides to his guest Marvy that he hopes one day to take these boys to Hollywood, where Cecil B. DeMille will use them as singers. Marvy points out that it's more likely that DeMille will want to use them as galley slaves in an epic film about the Greeks or Persians. Chiclitz is outraged: "Galley slaves? . . . Never, by God. For DeMille, young fur-henchmen can't be rowing!"

Here are three riffs on the same line, the first a frequently cited feghoot, the latter two dreamed up by your author. The setups are mercifully abridged from the usual preambles that may go on for days.

A zoologist discovered a new species of creature in the English county of Kent, and because of its uniqueness, he named it a "Rarie." Small at first, the Rarie had a voracious appetite and grew to a very large size. One day the Rarie, now enormous and a threat to human beings, escaped from its cage and headed toward the white cliffs of Dover, where it hovered on the rim. The public was alarmed and the British Army was sent in to destroy the Rarie by toppling it over the edge of the cliffs into the channel. To do so, a complicated weighted pulley system was devised, in which the Rarie would be attached to a crane, and a weight would then be removed to force the Rarie over the cliff. The Army had this all set up to go, when the zoologist arrived on the scene and realized the device would not work. As he told the soldiers: "It's a wrong weight to tip a Rarie."

In another version, an office manager hires a temp from an agency. When she arrives for an interview, the manager is busy, so his secretary tells her to have a seat. When the manager finally is able to see her, he asks her how long she has been there. "Seven hours," she replies. "It's a long wait for a temporary."

And, finally (you will no doubt be glad to hear): Nobel Prize winner Al Gore's wife invited Barbra Streisand to visit her in a vacation cabin at the top of one of Tennessee's Great Smoky Mountains. Streisand was told that the trek up the mountainside was long and treacherous, so to keep up her spirits she decided that she would sing some Top 40 songs. And so she sang hits along the way to a Tipper aerie.

Enough (perhaps far too much?) said on that subject.

—•—

A man was divorced three times and complained to his lawyer that he was never free from his former wives' constant demands for alimony. His lawyer said, "Well, everyone knows the ties of exes are upon you."

—•—

The following story, which is believed to have originated with members of the Seattle Symphony Orchestra, but has received many embellishments over time, might be regarded as a prime example of the feghoot form. During the performance of Beethoven's Ninth Symphony there is a long passage during which the bass violins have nothing to play. After playing their parts in the early passages of the

Symphony, it was the custom of the bass section to leave the stage and wait in the wings until their reentry, at the beginning of the last movement. On one occasion the bass players decided they had time to step across the street to a bar for a drink. They had a couple of rounds and one of them said, "Shouldn't we get back? It'd be embarrassing to be late." "Don't worry," said another. "I tied a string around a page in the conductor's score that comes just before our part, and I'm holding the other end of the string, so when he turns the page, I'll feel the tug."

So they had another round of drinks and, sure enough, a few minutes later, the bass-player felt the string tug, and they returned to the stage, by this time pretty tipsy—in fact, two of them passed out in their chairs. The others saw that the conductor had stopped before the last movement so that a violinist, whose name was Herman Batter, could retune his instrument. He was standing, waiting for the oboe to give him an "A." So the situation was this: It was the last of the Ninth, the score was tied, the basses were loaded, two men were out, Batter was up and waiting for the pitch.

Of a similarly elaborate nature—some people might even say far more trouble than it is worth—is the prefatory setup required for the following story: An aquarium keeper discovered that his dolphins could live forever if he fed them a diet of mynah birds and lion steaks. His food supplier had no trouble in acquiring sufficient birds, but the only nearby lions were in a preserve on the estate of a wealthy naturalist. The supplier loaded his truck with mynahs and on the way to the aquarium decided he would try to abduct some of the lions as he passed the estate. The lions, understandably, were made somewhat ill-tempered by this prospect. The scheme, however, came to naught when the

food supplier was arrested by federal authorities and charged with a violation of the Mann Act. Why? For attempting to transport mynahs and cross estate lions for immortal porpoises.

Out of every two dozen squid, there's always one who does not know how to swim away quickly— but twenty-three squid do.

If feghoots are a bit much for you, you might prefer this naughty pun about Oscar Wilde, whose well-known same-sex preference was not in accord with Victorian mores. Wilde once promised a straitlaced friend that he would reform, and some while later the friend was dismayed to discover Oscar in a hotel room in bed with one of the hotel bellboys. "Oscar," the friend remonstrated, "you said you were going to turn over a new leaf." "Oh, I am, I am," replied Oscar, "just as soon as I get to the bottom of the page."

Nothing succeeds like excess.
—Oscar Wilde

Then there were the identical twin boys who were separated at birth, one sent to foster parents in Mexico, where he was given the name Juan, and the other to a Middle Eastern country, where he was called Amahl. An international agency tried to arrange an adoption to reunite them with one family. They sent a photograph of Juan to a couple who were interested in adopting both boys. The couple wrote back, asking to see a photograph of the other boy. The agency replied: "They're twins. When you've seen Juan, you've seen Amahl."

———◆———

The upholsterer who had an accident and fell into his machine is now fully recovered.

———◆———

———◆———

Author's note to self: *To avoid a hostile and possibly dangerous uprising by readers, better stop here and move on to something else.*

———◆———

For the few of you masochists who are not sated yet, try this Web site for thousands of "quite awful" puns: pages.city2000.net

Oh, what the heck, just one more. A newspaper headline proclaimed: ENERGIZER BUNNY ARRESTED—CHARGED WITH BATTERY.

CHAPTER TWO

RISQUÉ BUSINESS

Clerihews and Limericks

Edmund Clerihew Bentley
Worked swiftly if not gently,
Tracking murderers down by a hidden clew
In whodunit and clerihew.

—Edmund Clerihew Bentley

Lots of people, especially rich and powerful ones, have cities, buildings, even stars named in their honor, but how many are forever known by the name of a verse form? Let's see, there's the Petrarchan sonnet, the Shakespearean sonnet, the Spenserian stanza—and the clerihew. E. C. Bentley, who died in 1956 at the age of eighty, was a British novelist and journalist much admired by Dorothy L. Sayers for his intricate detective stories featuring Inspector Trent, and by G. K. Chesterton for the invention of a verse form—the clerihew—that bears his middle name. Clerihew is an old Scottish name, the origin of which is unclear, and the largest concentration of the family is in Aberdeenshire. The name became attached to the four-line verses because in 1905 Bentley published a volume of them, called *Biography for Beginners*, under the name E. Clerihew.

A clerihew typically is a gently humorous four-line verse, with an AABB rhyme scheme, about a notable person whose name ends the first line. The second line makes a statement about the person and rhymes with the name. The third and fourth lines develop some aspect of the person's life or career, usually in a whimsical manner. No particular meter is mandated, and in fact, it is sometimes metrically irregular on purpose for comic effect. This aspect of the verse was satirized in a clerihew by an unknown wag:

> Edmund Clerihew Bentley
> Was evidently
> A man
> Who couldn't get his poems to scan.

Bentley invented the verse form when he was a sixteen-year-old student at St. Paul's School in London. One day he became bored during a chemistry class (well, who except a chemist would blame him?) and idly wrote the following, much to the amusement of his fellow students:

> Sir Humphry Davy
> Was not fond of gravy.
> He lived in the odium
> Of having discovered sodium.

After that, there was no stopping young Edmund (and some people no doubt tried). By the time he was thirty, with a degree from Oxford (where else?) in his pocket, he had cranked out enough of his four-line verses to make a book, including the following:

Sir Christopher Wren
Said, "I am going to dine with some men.
If anyone calls
Say I am designing St. Paul's."

John Stuart Mill,
By a mighty effort of will,
Overcame his natural bonhomie
And wrote *Principles of Economy*.

What I like about Clive
Is that he is no longer alive.
There is a great deal to be said
For being dead.

Edward the Confessor
Slept under the dresser.
When that began to pall,
He slept in the hall.

It was a weakness of Voltaire's
To forget to say his prayers,
And one which to his shame
He never overcame.

A few other historically notable examples of the form must include:

Daniel Defoe
Lived a long time ago.
He had nothing to do, so
He wrote *Robinson Crusoe*.

George the Third
Ought never to have occurred.
One can only wonder
At so grotesque a blunder.

Edgar Allan Poe
Was passionately fond of roe.
He always liked to chew some,
While writing anything gruesome.

"No, Sir," said General Sherman,
"I did not enjoy the sermon;
Nor I didn't git any
Kick outer the litany."

—◆—

Other irrepressible practitioners of the clerihew include Bentley's
friend Chesterton, J. R. R. Tolkien, and W. H. Auden—as well as
the author of this volume, who assumes total responsibility for the
following batch.

As he reveled with pals, F. Scott Fitzgerald
Fretted that his book sales had become imperiled.
He thought, "I'd better let all these aristocrats be,
And get busy and finish *The Great Gatsby*."

In the midst of his sentences, Henry James
Was sometimes muddled about his aims.
His lofty thoughts were quite resplendent,
But his clauses were frequently too independent.

The social realist Theodore Dreiser
Was also occasionally a womanizer.
When his libido got loose and he couldn't catch it, he
Considered it *An American Tragedy*.

His prying neighbors said that William Faulkner
Had a long-haired dog, and when he was walkin' her,
She'd bark and shed her hair in a flurry.
So Faulkner called her *The Sound and the Furry.*

When Nobel Prizes were given, it would make Graham Greene
With envy to see the winners preen.
He'd get mad as a hatter,
And that was really *The Heart of the Matter.*

A crotchety satirist was Evelyn Waugh
And as dauntless a man as you ever saw.
It's surprising that his best work all
Came after his *Decline and Fall.*

Jean-Paul Sartre
Always ordered à la carte.
He'd say "nix"
To the prix fixe.

Papa Ernest Hemingway
Never wrote books in the Ian Fleming way.
The guns of 007 for him held no charms,
That's why he said *A Farewell to Arms.*

T. S. Eliot
Took his tea, toast, and jelly at
Exactly eight by his new clock,
Then he wrote "The Love Song of J. Alfred Prufrock."

Robert Frost
In a forest was lost.
But, *entre nous,*
Whose woods they were he thought he knew.

James Joyce
Laughed so hard he lost his voice
When the censors had several hissies
While reading *Ulysses*.

Leonard Bernstein
Was playing on Jerome Kern's Stein-
-way. But it gave him a pain in the liver
Because all it would play was "Ol' Man River."

Maestro Serge Koussevitzky,
Couldn't get his band to play in Eartha Kitt's key.
He said to her: "You can call me a whiner,
But though your talent may be major—the key is minor."

Frank Lloyd Wright
Once fell in love—and at first sight.
But then he and she fought, and though he was bereft,
And she was wrong, all right—Wright left.

Two architects whose name was Saarinen
Wanted to invite the singer Bobby Darin in.
They loved his music; he was a hero
Both to Eliel and to Eero.

The architect Ralph Adams Cram
Thought one employee not worth a damn.
The employee was fired—and to his dismay,
Learned too late that Cram doesn't pay.

Mies van der Rohe
Said, "Gosh, my cash is running low.
My taxes are so high, I guess,
When I earn more, then more is less."

Le Corbusier
Crowed, "My last design was a doozy, eh?"
After erecting a few skyscrapers,
He'd always look for his name in the papers.

If Clark Gable
Had known his movies would be shown on cable,
He would have been among those individuals
Demanding higher residuals.

Marlene Dietrich
Could do a neat trick:
Singing Lutheran hymns
While flaunting her legendary limbs.

Sir Noël Coward
Shaved and showered,
Had coffee and a prune,
Then wrote a song in the morning and a play in the afternoon.

Bob Hope
Said, "Nope—
I don't care if he can sing,
I won't make another picture with Bing."

Bing Crosby
Said, "No matter what his flaws be,
For me it's no prob
To do another picture with Bob."

When General George Washington
Got all his joshing done,
He'd sometimes think of that one tree
He cut down before becoming Father of His Country.

Thomas Jefferson
Raised horses and heifers, son—
But mostly his descendants
Were grateful that he wrote the Declaration of
    Independence.

Dropping his "g's," Abraham Lincoln
Said "hopin'" and "thinkin,'"
But no one thought any the less
Of his Gettysburg Address.

- - - - -

It's more than likely that by now you've had your fill of clerihews. But this is a double-barreled chapter of verse, and you're about to be under attack by a second volley coming from the limerick. As everyone probably knows, a limerick is a five-line verse, with a rhyme scheme of AABBA, with three metrical feet in the first, second, and fifth lines, and two in the third and fourth. The subject matter is almost always humorous, and apart from the squeaky-clean oeuvre of Edward Lear, the man who popularized the form, and a very few other practitioners, it is usually obscene to a greater or lesser degree.

Unlike the clerihew, whose origin can be pinned down to a precise time, place, and person, the limerick came to life in the mists of obscure antiquity. Presumably it has something to do with the city or county of Limerick in Ireland, but no one seems to know quite what. *The Oxford English Dictionary*, in the best tradition of equivocation, suggests that it might have originated in "convivial" parties in Ireland, at which it was customary for the guests, at the height of their conviviality, to compose (probably salacious) humorous verses that ended with a raucously sung refrain whose last line was "Will you come up to Limerick?" But remember, this is mere conjecture. And while no one can swear to it on a stack of dictionaries, the first documented use of the word to describe a verse form is thought to be in the title of an 1898 book—*Illustrated Limericks*.

Although they were not called limericks until the dawn of the twentieth century, verses of that sort were associated with the Irish locale a few hundred years earlier through a group known as the Maigue Poets, who clustered about the town of Croom, on the River Maigue, in County Limerick. Among early examples of verses in limerick form were a matching pair written in the eighteenth century by the Maigue poets Sean O'Tuama and Andrias MacCriath. O'Tuama ran a pub, and perhaps this verse was meant as an advertisement for his wares:

> I sell the best brandy and sherry
> To make all my customers merry,
> But at times their finances
> Run short as it chances,
> And then I feel very sad, very.

MacCriath fired back this reply:

> O'Tuama! You boast yourself handy
> At selling good ale and bright brandy,
> But the fact is your liquor
> Makes everyone sicker,
> I tell you this, I your good friend, Andy

In *The Lure of the Limerick*, a trove of admirably scabrous examples of the verses, luridly illustrated by decadent Aubrey Beardsley drawings, William S. Baring-Gould makes an effort to pin down the history of the limerick with some precision. Baring-Gould cites F. A. Wright's book *Greek Social Life*, in which a verse in limerick form is attributed to the jocund Aristophanes in his play *The Wasps*.

Be that as it may, it all being Greek to your unilingual author, one stanza of the Middle English poem "Summer is i-cumen in," which dates from around 1300, is unquestionably in limerick form, lacking only a perfect rhyme pattern:

> Ewè bleateth after lamb,
> Low'th after calfè cow;
> Bullock starteth,
> Buckè farteth,
> Merry sing, cuckoo!

The limerick form reappeared in the seventeenth century in the anonymously written song "Tom o'Bedlam," a verse of which goes:

> From the hagg and hungrie goblin
> That into raggs would rend ye,

And the spirit that stands
By the naked man,
In the Booke of Moones defend ye.

Shakespeare also dabbled in the limerick form, in several of his plays. In *Hamlet* the mad Ophelia laments the perfidy of men in a ribald near-limerick:

By Gis [Jesus] and by Saint Charity,
Alack and fie for shame!
Young men will do't,
If they come to't,
By Cock, they are to blame.

And in *Othello* Iago sings a limerick-like drinking ballad:

And let me the canakin clink, clink
And let me the canakin clink.
A soldier's a man,
O man's life's but a span;
Why, then, let a soldier drink.

——◆——

The first known book of limericks, though not by that name—*The History of Sixteen Wonderful Old Women*—was published in 1821 in London by John Harris. As one of the sixteen is described therein:

There was an old woman of Leeds,
Who spent all her life in good deeds.
She worked for the poor
Till her fingers were sore,
This pious old woman of Leeds.

You will notice immediately that the first and last lines do not rhyme; they end with the same word. This practice was customary in nineteenth-century limericks and especially in the verses of the man who made the form popular, Edward Lear. However the limerick may have begun, it was Lear who launched it on its seemingly unstoppable career in two books of nonsense verse, the first in 1845 and a later one in 1872. Lear, who is also noted for such non-limerick works as "The Owl and the Pussycat," "The Jumblies," and "The Pobble Who Has No Toes," said he was inspired to write in the limerick form by a verse he had read in a follow-up to Harris's book, *Anecdotes and Adventures of Fifteen Gentlemen*, which was published in 1822 by John Marshall and included a verse that recounted:

> There was a sick man of Tobago,
> Who liv'd long on rice-gruel and sago;
> But at last, to his bliss,
> The physician said this—
> "To a roast leg of mutton you may go."

While Lear's poems generally followed an AABBA rhyme pattern, they are not always set in five lines of type. The verses were used as illustrations for pictures and set in whatever format was needed to fill the space. In all, Lear wrote 212 limericks, and if he wrote any that you couldn't read in a Sunday School class, they are unknown to your author. A few samples of his whimsical, innocuous verses would include the following, in which you will note that Lear favored limericks about old men:

There was an Old Man with a beard,
Who said, "It is just as I feared!
Two Owls and a Hen,
Four Larks and a Wren,
Have all built their nests in my beard!"

There was an Old Man in a tree,
Who was horribly bored by a Bee;
When they said, "Does it buzz?"
He replied, "Yes, it does!"
"It's a regular brute of a Bee!"

There was an Old Man of Kilkenny,
Who never had more than a penny;
He spent all that money,
In onions and honey,
That wayward Old Man of Kilkenny.

There was an Old Person whose habits,
Induced him to feed upon rabbits;
When he'd eaten eighteen,
He turned perfectly green,
Upon which he relinquished those habits.

There was an Old Man who supposed,
That the street door was partially closed;
But some very large rats,
Ate his coats and his hats,
While that futile old gentleman dozed.

There was a Young Lady whose chin,
Resembled the point of a pin;
So she had it made sharp,
And purchased a harp,
And played several tunes with her chin.

There was an Old Man of Moldavia,
Who had the most curious behaviour;
For while he was able,
He slept on a table.
That funny Old Man of Moldavia.

—◆—

A few classic post-Lear examples, whose authors remain unknown,
would include:

There was an old party of Lyme
Who married three wives at one time.
When asked, "Why the third?"
He replied, "One's absurd,
And bigamy, sir, is a crime!"

There was a young lady from Guam,
Who observed, "The Pacific's so calm
That there can't be a shark,
I'll just swim for a lark—"
Let us now sing the Twenty-third Psalm.

A gentleman dining in Kew
Found quite a large mouse in his stew.
Said the waiter: "Don't shout
And wave it about,
Or the others will all want one, too."

The *Princeton Tiger* printed a limerick in the early years of the twentieth century that spawned many of its ilk, some of them not as presentable in polite company as this one is:

> There was an old man of Nantucket,
> Who kept all his cash in a bucket.
> But his daughter, named Nan,
> Ran away with a man,
> And as for the bucket, Nantucket.

Later wags improved on it, first by a limerick in the *Chicago Tribune* followed by one in the *New York Press:*

> Pa followed the pair to Pawtucket,
> (The man and the girl with the bucket)
> And he said to the man,
> "You're welcome to Nan,"
> But as for the bucket, Pawtucket.

> Then the pair followed Pa to Manhasset,
> Where he still held the cash as an asset.
> And Nan and the man
> Stole the money and ran,
> And as for the bucket, Manhasset.

That old punster-physician Oliver Wendell Holmes, Sr., is credited with one of the most famous of the nineteenth-century limericks:

> Henry Ward Beecher, the preacher,
> Called a hen a most elegant creature,
> The hen, pleased with that,
> Laid an egg in his hat—
> And thus did the hen reward Beecher.

Mark Twain is known to have written at least one limerick, in which he plays with the orthography of a much-used abbreviation:

> A man hired by John Smith and Co.
> Loudly declared he would tho.
> Man that he saw
> Dumping dirt hear his store.
> The drivers, therefore, didn't do.

A similar feat was performed by Eugene Field, better known for "Wynken, Blynken, and Nod," "Little Boy Blue," and other sentimental poems, when he wrote (unsentimentally, but insensitively, of course, by today's standards):

> Now what in the world shall we dioux
> With the bloody and murderous Sioux,
> Who some time ago
> Took an arrow and bow
> And raised such a hellabelioux?

President Woodrow Wilson frequently quoted, although did not, as many people thought, actually write:

> As a beauty I'm not a great star,
> There are others more handsome by far,
> But my face, I don't mind it,
> Because I'm behind it—
> It's the folks in the front that I jar.

Another marvelous example, which not only illustrates the limerick but also contains an elegant pun, has appeared in several versions, among them:

There was a young fellow named Paul,
Who fell in the spring in the fall,
'Twould have been a sad thing
Had he died in the spring,
But he didn't—he died in the fall.

—◆—

As the limerick matured, it developed a libidinous will of its own and grew more racy in its content—in fact, so adult that most post-Lear examples would have to be R-rated and are decidedly unfit for consumption by certain segments of the population. In limerick form you might put it this way (you might, but it was your smart-alecky author who did):

The limerick is bold and audacious,
Coquettish and very flirtatious,
Not well-behaved,
In fact, most depraved,
And, more often than not, quite salacious.

Or, as another limericist, this one anonymous, would have it:

The limerick yields laughs anatomical
In a form that is quite economical,
And the good ones I've seen
Are so seldom clean,
And the clean ones are so seldom comical.

—◆—

Here is a sampling of elegant, though decidedly obscene limericks, excusable only because they are irresistibly funny—a defense of obscenity offered by no less an authority than U.S. Supreme Court Justice Antonin Scalia. None of the authors' names are known—for which most of them will thank their lucky stars.

There was a young fellow called Cyril,
Who was had in the wood by a squirrel,
And it felt so damn good,
He stayed in the wood
As long as the squirrel was virile.

A young lady went walking in Exeter,
And all the young men craned their necks at her.
There was one so depraved
That he actually waved
The distinguishing mark of his sex at her.

There was a young monk from Siberia,
Whose morals were rather inferior.
He did to a nun
What he shouldn't have done,
And now she's a Mother Superior.

On the breast of a floozy named Gail
Was tattooed the price of her tail,
While on her behind,
For the sake of the blind,
Was written the same thing, in Braille.

There was an old maid from Worcester,
Who dreamt that a man had seduced her,
But she found out instead
That a spring in her bed
Had poked through the mattress and goosed her.

A young student up at St. John's
One day tried to bugger the swans.
"No, no," said the porter,
"I'll give you my daughter—
But those swans are reserved for the dons."

———◆———

And finally, a few entries (as it were) from your very own author, with the hope that the ribaldry will not remain unforgiven and even more that it will not remain unread.

A right reverend monsignor named Xavier
Engaged in some shocking behavior.
He ravished a prior,
Three nuns, and a friar
Then knelt and gave thanks to the Savior.

There was a young man from Australia
Dismayed by his small genitalia.
He adorned them with leather,
Gold stars, and a feather,
And won prizes for all his regalia.

At the beach a gent from Toledo
Ogled a gal in a Speedo.
He liked both her suit,
Which he thought was quite cute,
And the way it aroused his libido.

Shakespeare provides the inspiration for the next group:

A lover of Lady Macbeth,
Paused a moment to just catch his breath.
But then Lady Mac
Said, "The thane's coming back,
Put your clothes on, or you'll catch your death."

One king of England, I've heard,
Was never a man of his word.
Moreover, I've found
When he wasn't around,
His friends called him Richard the Turd.

Two actors whose conduct was heinous
Said, "Even though it may strain us,
Since we're not well endowed,
Nonetheless we're quite proud
We've had small parts in *Coriolanus*."

And now the Final Four, as the college all-stars:

A bashful young coed at Baylor
Was afraid her professor would fail her.
She got over her shyness
And earned an A-minus
With some techniques she'd learned from a sailor.

A young English major at Brown
Offered phone sex of widespread renown.
She could moan the F-word
As her clients preferred,
As an adjective, adverb, or noun.

There was a young co-ed at Smith
For whom orgasm was only a myth.
At last she achieved it,
But no one believed it,
Including the guy she was with.

A theater major at Bard
In college productions was starred.
Her thespian arts
Thrived on nice juicy parts,
Preferably long and quite hard.

There are more, some of them even more highly lubricious, but we'd all turn beet-red with embarrassment, and some sensitive readers might faint dead away, were they to continue any longer in this vein. Suffice it to say, in closing, in the immortal words of some other, anonymous poet:

A young lady who was clearly no prude
Loved to go for a swim in the nude.
A man came along
And, unless I'm quite wrong,
You expected this line to be lewd.

CHAPTER THREE

LETTER RIP!

Lipograms, Univocalics, Anagrams, Palindromes, Charade Sentences, Rhopalics, Isoliterals, and Isosyllabics

Glow on, glow on, tiny star,
Your ID's not known so far.
Up so high, so truly high—
Twinkling diamond in our sky!

— Your author

You might be surprised by what some people do for fun. Now don't get excited—that's not a reference to the concupiscent shenanigans of the previous chapter. This chapter, teeming with much better behaved words—each of them, in fact, a *bon mot*—deals with a more arcane pastime: manipulating the letters in words by rearranging them, or omitting one or more of them in writing a document, or making them read identically backward and forward, or using progressively more or less of them in a sentence. These absurd practices, hold an inscrutable fascination for a tiny fraction of the world's populace. If you are not among that fraction, you will be mystified why anyone would devote so much effort to achieving such pointless feats. The reason is surely analogous to President John F. Kennedy's explanation of why folks climb Mount Everest or send a man to the moon: because it's there.

Lipogrammatists and others of that ilk do what they do because they can.

The making of lipograms—writing that purposely omits a certain letter of the alphabet—has a long history in literature. The word comes from the Greek *lipo*, meaning "lacking," plus *gramma*, meaning "something written or drawn." The first lipogram may have been an ode to centaurs by Lasus of Hermione (born 568 B.C.) in which the letter *sigma* was omitted, presumably because its sibilance was deemed unsuitable for poetry. Stephen Chrisomalis at his Web site phrontistery.info lists hordes of writers of lipograms, among the earliest of whom was Tryphiodorus, an Egyptian-born Greek, who around the fourth century A.D. chronicled Odysseus's journey in twenty-four books, each of which omitted one letter of the alphabet.

Then there's Gyles Brandreth, an impossibly versatile British jack-of-all-trades—biographer of Prince Charles and Camilla Parker Bowles, novelist, actor, broadcaster, children's book author, businessman, former Member of Parliament and lord commissioner of the treasury in John Major's government. He has rewritten several of Shakespeare's plays, each without a specific letter: *Hamlet* with no *I* ("To be or not to be, that's the query"), *Macbeth* with no *A* or *E*, and *Othello* without an *O*—the latter two feats most remarkable, inasmuch as the name of Macbeth, dragging its *A* and *E* with it, appears forty-two times in Shakespeare's text, and Othello, enclosed by its two *O*'s, makes twenty-four appearances.

You'll want to rush right out to tell your friends that the oldest known lipogram now extant is a sixth-century history of the world, *De Aetatibus Mundi et Hominus*, by one Fabius Planciades Fulgentius. As with Tryphiodorus, Fabius's scheme was to omit successive letters of the alphabet in each chapter, only fourteen of which still exist.

The modern master of lipograms is undoubtedly A. Ross Eckler, who lives in New Jersey (a state in which *E* is the only vowel), and who has a Princeton PhD in math. You'd need such a degree to comprehend fully some of the elaborate logological examples in his book *Making the Alphabet Dance*. One of Eckler's most prodigious feats is the rewriting of "Mary Had A Little Lamb" in several versions, preserving both sense and meter, successively without the letters *E* (the most frequently appearing letter in the English language), *S*, *H*, *T*, and *A*. Without an *E*, for example, Eckler changes "Mary had a little lamb, its fleece was white as snow" to "Mary had a tiny lamb, its wool was pallid as snow." (Sometimes you have to lose something of the meter.) The opening line of the version without a *T* is "Mary had a pygmy lamb, his fleece was pale as snow." And in the version without *A*, "Mary" has to become "Polly" and the "lamb," a "sheep."

The verse at the heading of this chapter is your author's attempt to do the same kind of thing—rewrite without an *E*—to "Twinkle, Twinkle, Little Star." The original, of course, goes:

> Twinkle, twinkle, little star,
> How I wonder what you are.
> Up above the world so high,
> Like a diamond in the sky.

Since the next most frequent letters in English are *T, A, O,* and *I*, it seemed mandatory to take the stunt a few steps further; hence, here are versions of "Twinkle, Twinkle, Little Star" without a *T*, without an *A*, without an *O*, without an *I*, and, finally, in burst of showy flamboyance, without an *E*, a *T*, an *A*, an *O*, or an *I*. No representations are made as to the resulting poetic quality—or, for that matter, as to simple intelligibility.

(WITHOUT *T*)

Shine on, smallish evening glow,
Who you are would I could know.
Up above our world so high,
Like a diamond in our sky.

(WITHOUT *A)*

Twinkle, twinkle, little glow,
Who you be I'd like to know.
Up over our world so high,
Glorious gemstone in the sky.

(WITHOUT *O)*

Twinkle, twinkle, little star,
Unidentified, afar,
Up in the ether very high,
Like a jewel in the sky.

(WITHOUT *I*)

Sparkle, sparkle, yon small star,
How we wonder what you are.
Above the world, where we can spy
You—gorgeous jewel of the sky.

(WITHOUT *E, T, A, O,* or *I*)

Burn, burn, puny sun!
Why, why, why run?
Hurry up—hug sky!
Ruby, huh? Uh-uh. My, my!

Well, that's that, and just be grateful there'll be no attempt to do it without any vowels at all.

Much more impressive lipograms are found in the work of the American Ernest Vincent Wright and the French writer Georges Perec, both of whom wrote entire novels—Wright's about 50,000 words, Perec's twice as long, and in French—without using the letter *E*. Wright called his book *Gadsby: Champion of Youth* (an allusion to Fitzgerald's *The Great Gatsby*), and, lamentably, on the very day of its publication in 1939, he died. Or perhaps it would be more appropriate to report the death of an *E*-less author by writing "that man did succumb with finality." *Gadsby* was reissued in 1997 by the Lightyear Press and is now apparently out of print. Rare used copies are sometimes available at amazon.com, and the entire text of the novel appears on a Web site called spinelessbooks.com. Wright explains his phenomenal achievement in an introduction (which does use the letter *E*, just to get it out of his system):

"The entire manuscript of this story was written with the E type-bar of the typewriter tied down; thus making it impossible for that letter to be printed. . . . As the vowel E is used more than five times oftener than any other letter, this story was written, not through any attempt to attain literary merit, but due to a somewhat balky nature, caused by hearing it so constantly claimed that 'it can't be done; for you cannot say anything at all without using E, and make smooth continuity, with perfectly grammatical construction'—so 'twas said. This has been accomplished through the use of synonyms; and, by so twisting a sentence around as to avoid ambiguity."

Judge for yourself, intrepid reader, how lucid the prose is with this sample from the first chapter:

"Now, in all such towns, you will find, occasionally, an individual born with that sort of brain which, knowing that his town is backward, longs to start things toward improving it; not only its living conditions, but adding an institution or two, such as any city, big or small, maintains, gratis, for its inhabitants. But so forward looking a man finds that trying to instill any such notions into a town's ruling body is about as satisfactory as butting against a brick wall. Such 'Boards' as you find ruling many a small town, function from such a soporific rut that any hint of digging cash from its cast iron strong box with its big brass padlock, will fall upon minds as rigid as rock."

Perec's *E*-less novel, written in 1969, is called *La Dispari-tion*, translated into English by Gilbert Adair, not literally as *The Disappearance*, which has three *E*'s, but as *A Void*, which avoids *E*'s with ease. In the novel the hero comes across a soliloquy by one William Shakspar that in its English translation might sound slightly familiar:

> *Living, or not living: that is what I ask:*
> *If 'tis a stamp of honour to submit*
> *To slings and arrows waft'd us by ill winds,*
> *Or brandish arms against a flood of afflictions,*
> *Which by our opposition is subdu'd?*

Like Wright of *Gadsby*, Perec also died young, at the age of forty-five.

Try writing a lipogram yourself. You'll probably find it a frustrating task, as your author did in constructing the following revisions of Abraham Lincoln's 278-word Gettysburg Address while trying to preserve both the sense and the style. As Wright confesses in his introduction to *Gadsby*, one often reaches a dead end in trying to express a given thought with synonyms for a forbidden word—and has to start the narrative process all over. The following versions of the Gettysburg Address are first the original, then as composed, successively, without *E*, *T*, or *A*. One could try this trick with every letter in the alphabet, but chances are there wouldn't be many readers after the first two or three, so let these examples suffice.

(The Original)

THE GETTYSBURG ADDRESS

Four score and seven years ago our fathers brought forth on this continent, a new nation, conceived in Liberty, and dedicated to the proposition that all men are created equal.

Now we are engaged in a great civil war, testing whether that nation, or any nation so conceived and so dedicated, can long endure. We are met on a great battle-field of that war. We have come to dedicate a portion of that field, as a final resting place for those who here gave their lives that that nation might live. It is altogether fitting and proper that we should do this.

But, in a larger sense, we can not dedicate—we can not consecrate—we can not hallow—this ground. The brave men, living and dead, who struggled here, have consecrated it, far above our poor power to add or detract. The world will little note, nor long remember what we say here, but it can never forget what they did here. It is for us the living, rather, to be dedicated here to the unfinished work which they who fought here have thus far so nobly advanced. It is rather for us to be here dedicated to the great task remaining before us—that from these honored dead we take increased devotion to that cause for which they gave the last full measure of devotion—that we here highly resolve that these dead shall not have died in vain—that this nation, under God, shall have a new birth of freedom—and that government of the people, by the people, for the people, shall not perish from the earth.

(WITHOUT *E*)
LINCOLN'S TALK AT A WAR DISTRICT

Long ago our patriarchs brought forth on this body of land an innovation among nations, born in individual rights, and sworn to a notion that all mankind had similar origins.

Now a major civil war is upon us, daring this nation, with such a birth and such a dogma, to last as long as it can. All of us now join in convocation in a combat district of that war. Our goal is to transform a portion of this district into a final tomb for troops lost fighting in this war district so that our nation might go on. It is totally right for us to do this.

But it is important to know that it is not within our grasp to truly hallow this ground. Such valiant troops, both living and lost, who fought in this district put upon it an aura of sanctity that is lacking in our poor ability to add or subtract. This world will not think much of what is said by us at this instant in this war district, but it cannot fail to think of what our valiant troops did. It is up to us living folks to commit to finish this fight so nobly fought so far. It is up to us to commit to a big task awaiting us—to light a lamp of ongoing duty to a dogma for which many of our valiant troops, now not living, fought and lost all. It is our duty to commit to our valiant missing troops that what was lost was not lost in vain; that it is our holy oath that this nation, with God's aid, is born again to committing to individual rights; and to a polity of all humanity, by all humanity, and for all humanity that shall not vanish from this world.

(WITHOUT *T*)
LINCOLN'S ADDRESS ON A PENNSYLVANIA FIELD

Fourscore and seven years ago, our founders began in our New World a new land and idea of governance, conceived in freedom and embracing fully a belief in all people's having been made equal.

Now we are engaged in a major civil war, and we are wondering if such a new idea of governance, so conceived and so pledged, can long endure. We are assembled here on a large field where a major skirmish of our war occurred. We have come here for hallowing a small area of ground as a final grave for soldiers who gave up life so our idea of governance could live. Doing so is very proper.

In a larger sense, however, we are powerless in hoping we can hallow such a piece of ground. Brave men, living and dead, who served nobly here, have hallowed such an area far beyond our poor power of adding or removing. Our world will have small remembrance of our sayings here; people, however, will never fail in recalling brave deeds done here. We who are living should pledge ourselves in finishing a grand work remaining before us—from our honored dead we derive increased hope in a cause for which lives were given—and we here highly resolve a promise ensuring our dead have died for good reason—and moreover, our idea of governance of people, by people, and for people shall always remain in our world.

—◆—

(WITHOUT *A*)

THE GETTYSBURG SPEECH

Ten hundred forty-four months previously, our founders brought forth on this continent this new country, conceived in liberty, pledged to the proposition of every person's being just like every other person.

Now we find ourselves in huge civil hostility, testing whether our country, so conceived, not to mention so pledged, will long endure. We find ourselves here on ground where much fighting occurred during this hostility. We come to invest some portion of this field with holiness for the serene repose of those who lost their lives so this country might live. It is completely fitting for us to do this.

But in truth we do not possess the power to turn this field into holy ground. The noble men, whether living or forever gone, who struggled here turned it into holy ground beyond our poor power to do so. The world will little note nor long remember the things we utter here, but it will never forget the things they did here. It is for us, the living, to be here committed to the big job lying before us—from these honored souls we derive more devotion to the proposition for which they delivered their full devotion—further, we here highly pledge to these men our word: their loss will not be fruitless—moreover, our country, under God, will be reborn in freedom, with government of the people, by the people, for the people never perishing from the world.

—•—

Author's note to self: Explore a possible connection between the concoction of lipograms and the untimely deaths of their authors.

—•—

A similarly pointless creation is the univocalic, a piece of writing using only one vowel—like the phrases "street scene" or "sci-fi" or "hat stand." Old friend Perec was also a devotee of this form of wordplay. One tour de force of his was a short story of almost five hundred words with the English title "What A Man," composed using only one vowel—the *A*. It dealt with a couple of pals named Andras MacAdam and Armand d'Artagnan.

Now, to be really daring, your author will attempt to create his own series of reasonably lucid sentences—depending on how you define "reasonably" or "lucid" or, for that matter, "sentences"—each of which uses only a single vowel:

(WITH ONLY *A*)

Alas, Hank, that sad Atlanta batsman, can't swat standard alfalfa. Alan, a gallant fat man that ran fast, can catch and slam balls at vacant

All-Star parks as mad fans, aghast, bark flagrant catcalls. What bald lad wants straw Panama hats—past stars' blatant garb à la La-La Land?

(WITH ONLY *E*)

Jeepers, creepers, where'd she get them peepers? She's been seen between three serene regent-pretenders. Mere speech vexes these esteemed shepherdesses, when terse teen revelers get the best red Celebes beets even when needed elsewhere. Greet seven green men— cheered, then dejected, when electees' deserted levees prevented sweet desserts.

(WITH ONLY *I*)

Did timid Sir Willis, giggling with bliss, hit it big, lining ill-fitting mini-bikini skirts with shining iris gris-gris fins, winning six-shillings in Fiji bills in tips, smiling whilst wiggling his impish hips? I'm dining with him in Rimini this night. I dig his thrilling picnic hijinks, mimicking vivid chi-chi civic flings: civilizing gin fizz first, with crisp British chips, insipid chili dips, mild shrimp grits, wild kingfish, finishing with simplistic fig-kiwi blinis.

(WITH ONLY *O*)

Oh, no, look how soon motors of most good old hobo robots go to pot. So who took Tom O'Connor's good rococo Botox tools to go on posh donors' hollow booths? Now, look—follow protocol—don't drop gold spoons, forks, bowls, pots, or combs—not down low on cold floors. Show both poor monks' photos from Kokomo's cool school books. Honor folks who grow cotton bolls. No polo from two o'clock on!

(WITH ONLY *U*)

Plump slum guru Hugh Duff usurps much surplus stuff—Zulu drums, pub mugs, stun-gun butts, full gum jugs, kudzu pulp, snuff urns, gnus' tusks, nuns' church cups, truck lugs, sump pumps, blunt clubs, thumb plugs, burnt tutus, bulb mulch, tux studs, fur trunks, unstrung rugs, Ruth Sununu's muumuus, U Nu's bust, bums' duds—plus tubs, slugs, pucks, skunks—ugh!—junk, but fun! Hugh's curt, gruff chum, glum thug Russ Bush, funds lunch—rum punch, Mumm's Brut, plums, curds, nut crunch, spuds, mud bugs, bulgur-durum sub buns—just

grub. Duff's dumb puss, Lulu, purrs. Bush's Pug pup, Lum, runs. Such susurrus! Such rumpus! Such tumult! Such ruckus!

And, finally, a feat only a fool (hello, there!) would try, creating alleged sentences using only that shifty vowel *Y*.

Shy? Why cry, sylphy ghyll nymph? Fly by thy Y's gym. Try hymn rhythms, wry trysts, dry myrrh, crypt glyphs, syzygy myths. My, my, my sly gypsy—psych pygmy spy!

Anagrams are another matter, for which you can use as many vowels as you like. They're one more thing you can thank the Greeks for, as if there weren't enough already. The word comes from the Greek *anagrammatismos*, meaning "transposition of letters." The game here is to rearrange the letters in a given word or group of words to form other words. One of the earliest anagrams was uttered (so it is alleged in Latin lore) in a colloquy between Pontius Pilate and Jesus Christ. *Quid est veritas?* ("What is truth?"), asked Pilate, and the answer was, *Est vir qui adest* ("It is the man who is here").

The simplest way to play anagrams is just to take a word and see how many other words can be made from the same letters. VEIL is a good example, which can also yield VILE, EVIL, and LIVE—

plus LEVI and LIEV if proper names are permitted. You can sometimes even make the semblance of a sentence or at least the staccato syntax of a newspaper headline out of a single anagrammatic word: RATS! ARTS TSAR TARS STAR, which one could (if backed to the wall) take to mean, "Doggone it, the government's cultural chief has made unflattering allegations about a leading performer." It gets trickier and more fun when you use more letters. If you try very, very hard, you can probably make some rudimentary sense out of these basic anagrams:

> CHASTE CHEATS SCATHE SACHET
>
> REDUST—RUDEST DUSTER RUSTED
>
> PASTIER PIRATES TRAIPSE PARTIES
>
> LISTEN—SILENT INLETS ENLIST TINSEL
>
> PASTEL PLEATS STAPLE PLATES' PALEST PETALS
>
> SPRIEST PRIESTS, SPRITES PERSIST: STRIPES, ESPRITS
>
> PADRES PARSED SPREAD DRAPES, RASPED, SPARED SPADER

More complex anagrams may rearrange the letters of a word or words into other multiple words. In the cleverest of them, the reformed letters relate in some way to the original. For example, among memorable classic anagrams are: DORMITORY ("dirty room"), ASTRONOMERS ("moon starers"), ASTRONOMICAL OBSERVATIONS ("to scan a visible star or moon"), FRENCH REVOLUTION ("violence run forth"), A GENTLEMAN ("elegant man"), and PRESBYTERIANS ("best in prayers," or, if you prefer, "Britney Spears").

Some anagrammatists like to take the names of newspapers and rearrange them to provide some amusing combination of relevant words, the more outrageous, the better. For example: *The New York Times* becomes "the monkeys write"; *The Scotsman*, "hasn't cost me"; *Cincinnati Post,* "ants picnic on it"; *Houston Chronicle,* "run hot cliché soon"; *The Washington Post,* "news photos at night."

Celebrities' names also offer fodder for anagrams. Julia Roberts might be "a sultrier job"; Jim Carrey yields "mercy! I jar"; Paris Hilton, "lost hairpin" or "hi, pal, I snort"; Tom Cruise provides a wealth of more or less apt anagrams: "so I'm cuter," "erotic sum," "oust crime," "omit curse," "I, costumer," "rue sitcom," "um, I escort," "ice or smut," "Mr., I use cot," "I so curt? Me?," "rout! sic 'em," and "I, Tom, curse." Who knew Tom Cruise could be so much fun?

One of the most remarkable anagrams ever created is a sonnet of sorts, fourteen rhymed, more-or-less metrical lines that mostly make sense, entitled "Washington Crossing the Delaware," each line of which is an anagram of the title. The provenance of the poem is mixed; some of the individual lines appeared in publications as early as 1879. The full version, in a slightly different form from the one printed here, is generally attributed to David Shulman in the June 1936 issue of *The Enigma.*

WASHINGTON CROSSING THE DELAWARE

A hard, howling, tossing water scene,
Strong tide was washing hero clean.
How cold! Weather stings as in anger.
O silent night shows war ace danger.
The cold waters swashing on in rage,
Slow Redcoats warn, his hint engage.[1]
Gen'l. W.'s reaction was this: "Harden, go!"[2]
He saw his ragged continentals row.
He stands while a tar crew's ongoing,[3]
And so this general watches rowing.
He hastens—winter again grows cold;
A wet crew gain Hessian stronghold.

George's hands can't lose war within;[4]
He's astern—so go, alight, crew, and win!

Four lines, indicated by footnotes above, were altered slightly by your author. The original lines in Shulman's version were:

[1]"Redcoats warn slow his hint engage."
[2]When general's star action wish'd "Go!"
[3]Ah, he stands—sailor crew went going,
[4]George can't lose war with's hands in;

All right, some of the lines don't make complete idiomatic sense, even the four rearranged from the original into what seemed to be slightly better syntax. Nonetheless, Mr. Shulman and his predecessors deserve acclaim—in kind, of course—so here are a few words of praise from your author, all anagrams of "Washington Crossing the Delaware":

Wow! Grand heights! It's so near clean.
No shit, whilst arcane words engage.
Writing a charade logs hot newness.
These wordings can win hearts' goal.

Let's settle for: Oh, a wit's wording enchants, regales!

-•◆•-

A palindrome, which everyone knows from "Able was I ere I saw Elba," is a word or sentence whose sequence of letters (or numbers) reads the same forward as backward. As might be expected, it comes from a Greek word, *palindromos*, which means, appropriately enough, "running back again." Greeks and Romans reveled in them, and among the first palindromes in English was a 1614 effort by John

Taylor (with the era's typical casual spelling): "Lewd I did live & evil did I dwel." An early palindrome that occurred naturally in real life  dates from 1866 and was the "Yreka Bakery"; yes, that's how the California town spells its name. "Madam, I'm Adam" and "Dennis sinned" are reasonably short ones that make good sense, but the attempt to construct lengthy ones usually results in little more than gibberish.

Dmitri Borgmann, Howard Bergerson, Jeff Grant, J. A. Linden, and Leigh Mercer are among noted palindromists (could that possibly be an actual profession?) of the modern era. The illustrious James Thurber was made even more illustrious by his classic "He goddam mad dog, eh?" A Web site called mockok.com (get it?) offers its judgment of the one hundred best English palindromes, and an even longer list can be viewed at brainyplanet.com. Some of their elegant examples are:

* Was it a rat I saw?
* Now ere we nine were held idle here, we nine were won.
* Reviled did I live, said I, as evil I did deliver.
* I saw desserts, I'd no lemons, alas, no melon, distressed was I.
* A man, a plan, a canal—Panama! (by Leigh Mercer)
* Sums are not set as a test on Erasmus. (by Leigh Mercer)
* Doc, note I dissent. A fast never prevents a fatness. I diet on cod. (by Peter Hilton or Penelope Gilliatt)
* Nurse, I spy gypsies—run!
* Drab as a fool, as aloof as a bard.

That Frenchman Perec—him again!—was also a fan of palindromes, and he created one of more than 1,300 words, totaling

5,566 letters. Here's the way Perec's lengthy chef d'oeuvre, which appeared in 1973 in *Repris de La Littérature Potentielle*, opens (*en français*, of course):

> *Trace l'inégal palindrome. Neige. Bagatelle, dira Hercule.*

Hundreds of words later it ends with those same letters in reverse order:

> *[1]e lucre: Haridelle, ta gabegie ne mord ni la plage ni l'écart.*

You can gaze in awe at the entire gargantuan construction on several Web sites.

Now as to what sense it makes, that's another matter. Using remnants of college French and a dictionary, your author came up with this stab at a (nonpalindromic) translation of the first part:

"Trace the unequal palindrome. Snows. Trifle, Hercules will say."

And at the other end, chugging to its final destination, with those same letters in reverse, it makes this much sense:

" . . . the money: Haridelle, your underhand dealings bite neither the beach nor the variation."

Dazzling as a 1,300-word palindrome may be, others have gone even further in English. In 2002 Nick Montfort and William Gillespie published *2002: A Palindrome Story in 2002 Words*. The story takes place in the year of the title, which happens to be the last palindromic year until 2112. Will Thomas has a 5,000-word narrative called *A Gassy Obese Boy's Saga*; Lawrence Levine is credited with a palindromic novel of 31,957 words under the title *Dr. Awkward & Olson in Oslo*; and David Stephens is the author of *Satire:Veritas*, reputedly more than 50,000 words, but who's counting?

And then there some lazy wag's 40,000-word palindrome entitled "The Utterance of the Petulant Child," which consists of the word "Mom" repeated 40,000 times. It might as well go to infinity.

Lucidity, as you must have noticed, is not the strong point of palindromes. If you're willing to settle for gibberish, no problem! Your author, who is certainly not adventurous enough to attempt anything longer than what you could say in one breath, offers these modest, but no less ghastly, attempts of his own before moving rapidly on to something else:

* Stressed, he won straw Smith saw in mulatto men if on tub, but no fine Mott alumni wash Tim's warts now, eh? Desserts?
* Did Stan's ass alone retame rotten timed nabob and emit net, to remate Reno lass, as Nat's did?
* Do go now; I'm aimed on a reviled road; no hymn I meet; star rats teem in my Honda, or deliver an ode Miami won—O, God!

Related to the palindrome in some fashion, most likely illegitimate, is the charade sentence. Charades being a guessing game in which syllables of words are acted out, charade sentences are those in which the order of the letters is identical, but the syllables are reconstructed to form different words. Got it? Well, to illustrate, here are a few pairs of charade sentences for what they are worth, which is precious little:

> Pumpkin gestates on icecap—'tain't easy!
> Pump king estate so nice, Captain Teasy.
>
> Put into nests arson tools on tiresome ether.
> Putin tones tsars onto Olson tire, so meet her.

No mad star tantrum petering out—yes, caper over.
Nomads tartan trumpeter in gouty escape rover.

Sorry, they're not going to make any more sense no matter how many times you read them.

Rhopalics are to be considered next in this chapter, and not a moment too soon. It's another one of those purposeless word games in which people of a certain kind find pleasure. From the Greek, as you probably suspected, the word derives from *rhopalikos*, meaning "shaped like a club thicker at one end than the other." In rhetoric a rhopalic is a sentence in which each successive word has one more syllable (or, as it's played sometimes, one more letter) than the previous one. Here's an example of a rhopalic with increasing syllables:

* A lucid manager organizes unregenerate, uncooperative antiprohibitionists' incomprehensibility.

Doing it with letters yields:

* I am not sure angry people readily perceive happiness everywhere surrounding unencumbered, unpretentious schoolchildren.

You can also do it in reverse, with the longest word at the beginning of the sentence. First with syllables:

* Incomprehensibility underaccommodated eleemosynary institutional charitable requirements very well.

And then a reverse rhopalic in which each word has one fewer letter than the last:

* Antiestablishment ophthalmologists, unsophisticated cosmetologists, perspicacious ditchdiggers, persnickety waitresses—generally everyone usually speaks words like you or I.

Some variations on this harmless, though intellectually questionable, activity are constructions of whole paragraphs consisting of words that have either the same number of letters or the same number of syllables. The semicoherent literary slumgullions that result from this time-wasting exercise might be called, respectively, isoliterals and isosyllabics, although your author can find no such definitions even in the tiny print at the bottoms of the dictionary pages. Perhaps it's just his myopia. Anyway, here are three paragraphs, the first a mind-numbing rant with words of only two letters, followed by only slightly less deranged attempts with three and four letters. Incidentally, it may help if you imagine the first speaker's native language is an obscure dialect spoken only in some remote enclave.

* Hi! Oh, Al, Ed, me, or Pa (he, an ex of Ma)—we do up an ox, eh? Ow! Fe, fi, fo! Aw, ha, ha, ha—so, if I'm to go on, no ax be by us. Ho! Lo, my id—he is at it, as in an ad. Ta!

* Mom may run far and buy ham, pea pie, hot tea, and jam, but not rum, gin, rye, egg nog, ale, and pop. Who can pay arm and leg for big tab? Yes, it's you! Aha—now all sit, gab, sip, and sup! Wow! See, how few are fat. Set one tan bib, new pan, pot lid, and pub cup per man. Dog and cow eat wee bit, yet pig and rat get zip. Has our boy let cat out? Why let any hot dim sum rot? Was the odd nun fed? Mad cop? Old Jew? Did sad end irk and vex him? Too bad!

* Five very nice tiny cats purr, then meet with four huge, ugly, mean dogs that bark, just when dusk goes dark. Chin firm, head held high, nose down, mind calm, each sees eyes glow. Ears hear. Lips curl. Jowl juts. Neck arcs. More long

wild rows seem sure. Nine tall elms sway from hard wind. Full moon atop hill puts pale blue aura over bare road. Late hour runs fast. What does fate hold? Time will tell. Most feel that once fang hits claw, some will kick, bite, yowl, fall, turn tail, soon flee with soft paws hurt. They don't ever look back.

—•——•—

Not quite Hemingway, but getting there! For those readers who are still here and in their right minds (an oxymoron?), here is a similar extravaganza, this time with syllables instead of letters.

First, a paragraph with one-syllable words only:

* Sure, I had real work on hand, but it was not that hard. My goal: learn what makes film stars tick—a tough job, yes, but you know me—up to the task. So how could I dig up facts? First, see lots of show biz folks—script girls, best boys, press reps, prop guys, stunt men—oh, yes—shrinks, too. All of them know great stuff to fill a book. Next, check some profs in West Coast schools who taught them when they were young. Then read the fan mags, since most are filled with dirt. One more thing: Take trips near their home towns and find those who knew them as kids. At last, truth will out. Screen leads have the same traits as most of us—fear, joy, zeal, nerve—plus tons of angst, of course.

Two-syllable words only:

* Fragrant, showy flowers—thorny roses, simple daisies, leafy asters, vibrant pansies, stately tulips, Easter lilies, reddish poppies, even gorgeous orchids—brighten sidewalks throughout many major cities. Sometimes someone pauses, sniffing sweetly scented breezes, before going about pressing daily errands. Others enjoy viewing vivid rainbow colors: cheerful yellows, regal purples, thrilling scarlets, somber crimsons. Many hurried shoppers rarely bother stopping, moving instead swiftly onward, seeking only greedy hucksters' tawdry bargains, sadly snubbing lovely floral décor. Heedless office workers also often scurry headlong into dreary buildings, never seeing any fleeting beauty. Pity busy people without enough leisure, always rushing, never finding pleasure amid bustling urban traffic.

And for the finale, three-syllable words only:

* Seemingly straightforward, studious history professors frequently scrutinize primary documents covering important periods, carefully researching forgotten trivial happenings. Publishing erudite articles openly revealing hitherto undisclosed verities rapidly elevates instructors, normally providing definite advancement careerwise—including excellent preferment, expected promotions, generous salary increases, fancier offices, competent graduate assistants, possibly official deference whenever departments assemble. Ambitious immature faculty newcomers, however, commonly exhibit unwelcome, devious tendencies resembling animal aggression. Genuine modesty, unselfish honesty, mutual friendliness represent qualities notably discouraged surrounding serious scholarship. Numerous distinguished pedagogues completed terrible haphazard manuscripts, thereupon shamefully obtaining coveted positions, offering obscenely excessive perquisites. Unbiased

observers thoughtfully suggesting personnel policy restrictions ruefully encountered voluble objections.

If you want to try constructing a sentence composed of only four-syllable words, be my guest—perseverance undoubtedly effectuates victorious accomplishments triumphantly.

CHAPTER FOUR

THINKING INSIDE THE BOX

Crossword Puzzles

A FAMILIAR FORM OF MADNESS: Latest of the problems presented for solution by psychologists interested in the mental peculiarities of mobs and crowds . . . is created by what is well called the craze over crossword puzzles. Scarcely recovered from the form of temporary madness that made so many people pay enormous prices for mah jong sets, about the same persons are now committing the same sinful waste in the utterly futile finding of words the letters of which will fit into a prearranged pattern, more or less complex. This is not a game at all, and it hardly can be called a sport; it is merely a new utilization of leisure by those for whom it would otherwise be empty and tedious.

—New York Times, November 17, 1924

Beginning today, The *New York Times*
inaugurates a puzzle page.
—New York Times, February 15, 1942

My, my!—such a change of heart as the *New York Times* underwent in the years between 1924 and 1942 can only have been caused by the enormous popularity that crossword puzzles found with the newspaper-buying public. The first genuine puzzle in an American newspaper, the work of Arthur Wynne, an impish British expatriate from Liverpool, appeared in the *New York World* in 1913.

71

Primitive by today's standards—one answer (DOVE) is used twice, and some answers (NEIF and TANE, for example) are not words in general use—the puzzle nonetheless was the first of a series that attracted a growing public. Almost three decades later, the *New York Times* finally decided it was time to get down and go across. Today that stately newspaper is considered by many the gold standard for the madness, now become permanent, that afflicts many people in the United States. The *Times* reached the pinnacle of puzzledom under the watchful eyes of only four editors in almost seven decades: Margaret Farrar (1942–1969), Will Weng (1969–1977), Eugene T. Maleska (1977–1993), and Will Shortz, a word wizard who is the only person in the world to have earned a college degree in "enigmatology," a course that he devised for himself at Indiana University.

Some people regard working crossword puzzles as beneficial mental stimulation. Others fear it may be an addiction that is a mental disorder in itself. Certainly those who are driven, not just to solve the puzzles, but to go so far as to construct them, suffer from an even more advanced form of mental derangement. However you feel about it, there is no mistaking the fact that next to inaccurate weather forecasts, the inadvertent omission of the crossword puzzle from a daily newspaper elicits the largest number of outraged complaints from readers.

Word puzzles have been around for millennia. The Greeks played with anagrams, and the Romans developed an early form of the crossword puzzle, known as word squares. One such creation, which dates from 79 A.D., is known as the Rotas or Sator Square:

R O T A S
O P E R A
T E N E T
A R E P O
S A T O R

Not only does this word square read the same down as it does across, it also is palindromic and may be read backward, both vertically and horizontally. The square even makes a coherent sentence that means something like "Working the wheels occupies Arepo the planter," which the Romans interpreted to mean "God controls the universe." Your author tried to come up with his own five-word square, and this is what emerged:

T O S C A
O S C A R
S C O R E
C A R O N
A R E N A

No, you can't read this one backward, and if you insist on meaning, the most you're going to extract from it is "The Oscar-winning score for the film version of the opera *Tosca* is to be performed by Leslie Caron in some arena." Attempting one with six letters, rather than five, yields the following result, which weaves four Shakespearean

characters into a situation in which two of them seem to be repudi-
ating two others, one of whom is Ionian:

```
P O R T I A
O B E R O N
R E C A N T
T R A N I O
I O N I A N
A N T O N Y
```

As for seven-, eight-, and even nine-letter word squares, they have
been the Holy Grail since the publication of the first six-word square
in the magazine *Notes & Queries* in 1859. It read:

```
C I R C L E
I C A R U S
R A R E S T
C R E A T E
L U S T R E
E S T E E M
```

When you get into eight- and nine-word categories, you begin to find
extremely obscure words or little-known proper names. Ross Eckler
cites a couple of nine-squares in *Making the Alphabet Dance*, but they
resort to such words as REEDLESSE, SANTONATE, ECPHO-
NEMA, ROGERENES, and SANGSTERE—probably not part
of anyone's working vocabulary. Now that the use of computers has
been introduced into the game, the new quest is to find a perfect
ten-square, for which a support base of more than 350,000 words is
deemed to be required.

Word squares are the ancestors of today's crossword puzzles, the construction of which your author has been practicing for a good many years, with modestly satisfactory results—a few in the *New York Times*, long runs of many years with the *Los Angeles Times* (now *Chicago Tribune*) Syndicate and with *Performing Arts Magazine*, several Simon & Schuster crossword books, and most recently with *Equity News*, the monthly newspaper read by actors when they are not employed, which is most of the time.

It was as an actor, in a misspent earlier life, that your author began constructing crossword puzzles. During a season with a repertory company, the roles assigned became successively smaller in each play, leaving plenty of time to dawdle in the dressing room while waiting to make an entrance, utter a line or two, and then exit. Tiring of aimlessly working newspaper crosswords and then tossing them away, your author enlisted two fellow actors, both incorrigible crossword-solvers, to critique his own inventions. By the last play of the season—then with little more than a walk-on part— your author was frustrated in his theatrical aspirations, but reasonably adept at crossword construction.

Now, avid reader, you are in luck, for ten scintillating puzzles, all with themes dealing with wordplay, were uncovered by your author lurking in a little-used desk drawer. They have been freshly groomed, slicked up, and attired in their finest apparel, in which they now present themselves for your solving pleasure.

BYRD WATCHING

CROSSWORD PUZZLE NUMBER ONE

ACROSS

1 Official precious gem of Nevada
5 Org. that publishes *Animal Times*
9 Pahlavis of Iran
14 _____ Alto
15 Ardently enthusiastic
16 TV drama on NBC for eight seasons
17 Allay
18 Lacquered metalware
19 Sentient
20 Lookout for Russell?
23 Cheat with a check
24 Does a P.R. job on
25 Where messages can be posted to newsgroups
27 Govt. bureau since 1968
30 Haw intro
31 False alternative
32 Health care providers
34 Calendar innovation made by Julius Caesar
38 Tight tartan trousers
39 Greatest extent possible, for short
40 Uncanny
41 Legally restricted, as property inheritance
43 Speaker of "If music be the food of love, play on"
44 Accomplish perfectly
45 Prepare for war
46 Dols.' components
47 Chaperone
50 Robert and Alan of show business
52 *Play _____ It Lays* (Didion novel)
53 Shade of blue for Tim?
58 Robustness
60 Butcher's offering
61 Mushroom
62 Maria _____ (Mrs. Buddy) Holly
63 Dame with lilac hair
64 Fork component
65 Koussevitzky or Diaghilev
66 Coll. sci. course
67 Spotted

DOWN

1 Assn. based in Vienna
2 "I kid you not" TV figure
3 Furthermore
4 _____ State theaters
5 Suckers
6 Goolagong of tennis
7 They may be found on a bathroom floor
8 Diluted fruit juice beverages
9 Patty Hearst's kidnappers, for short
10 Sharp vision for Ethan?
11 Delon or Ducasse
12 Author of "The Outcasts of Poker Flat"
13 "How _____ It Is" (Marvin Gaye song)
21 St. Paul addressee
22 Stripper Tessie in the musical *Gypsy*
26 Hero from Metropolis
27 Pay to play
28 Change direction
29 Guitar feature
31 Beneke or Ritter
33 Farewell for Lynn?
34 Shaveling
35 Idle in British humor
36 Isn't incorrect
37 Old cars from Olds
39 Brooks of Broadway
42 Fabricator
43 First, second, or third, e.g.
45 Silas in *The Da Vinci Code*, for one
47 Joints
48 Serviceable
49 Kind of beaver
50 Domicile
51 AF or USMC NCOs
54 One of the Cassinis
55 Soprano Mills from Illinois
56 *The Wind Done _____* (Alice Randall novel)
57 Ifill of "Washington Week"
59 Charlotte of "The Facts of Life"

CHANGING COURSES

CROSSWORD PUZZLE NUMBER TWO

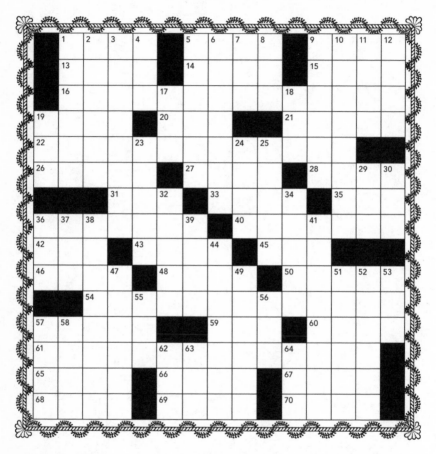

ACROSS

1 Male swans

5 Shakespeare sonnet that begins "Not mine own fears . . ."

9 Chrysalis

13 Frat Packer Wilson

14 St. Louis players previously in Cleveland and Los Angeles

15 Flavoring in 47-Down

16 Course on matter and energy that is confusing?

19 Dame of jazz singing

20 ____ Saud, first monarch of Saudi Arabia

21 Site of *My Fair Lady* Gavotte

22 Course on the life processes of pilots?

26 Davis who wrote and starred in *Purlie Victorious*

27 Award won by Lance Armstrong and Tiger Woods

28 Publisher who coined the phrase "All the news that's fit to print"

31 AEC's successor

33 Adolph Marx's instrument and most of his nickname

35 Name of 13 popes

36 Word on some cartons

40 Uses an iPod, perhaps

42 Punishment, in a saying

43 Per capita

45 Mazda or Lada

46 Over and above

48 Louis I–XVIII, e.g.

50 Desires

54 Course on points, lines, and angles in prisons?

57 The Jetsons' dog

59 Letters before Victory or Bounty

60 Controversial anthropologist who wrote *The Story of Man*

61 Course on roofing material through the ages?

65 "The most amazing thing ever invented," according to Rosie O'Donnell

66 Little hellion

67 "____ a very valiant rebel of the name": *Henry IV, Part I*

68 Copied the style of

69 Leap by Baryshnikov

70 Old Ford models

DOWN

1 Thick sauce on upscale menus

2 Capitalists and syndicalists

3 Flattering to one's appearance

4 NBC show since 1975

5 One of Malfoy's pals at Hogwarts

6 Boat's coat

7 Poe's "The ____ of the Perverse"

8 Kabibble of Kay Kyser's Kollege

9 Collect $200, perhaps

10 Circus parade vehicle

11 Neoplatonist ____ della Mirandola

12 Kind of prof.

17 Word before "Berliner" in a Kennedy speech

18 Ming on the court

19 Vietnamese religion ____ Dai

23 Fictional TV town in Indiana where odd events occurred

24 Gemstone with "church windows"

25 Type of soprano

29 Lobster or chicken

30 "Help!"

32 Barton or Bow

34 One of approximately 150 in the Bible

36 Lippo Lippi, for one

37 Poppycock

38 Kind of parent

39 Concern of EPA

41 Actual expense, no matter what the budget says

44 Snobbish

47 Drink that once contained absinthe

49 Arab or Hebrew

51 Put onto a CD-ROM

52 French city laid out in the shape of a champagne cork

53 Opp. of ant.

55 Holiday beverage

56 CIA forerunner

57 Charleses' dog

58 *Nina*, for one

62 Last U.S. president commonly referred to by his initials

63 Prior to in Prior

64 Theologian Cornelius Van ____

DISORDERLY CONDUCT

CROSSWORD PUZZLE NUMBER THREE

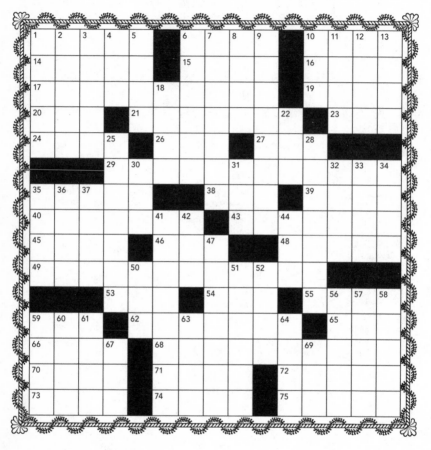

ACROSS

1 Was told
6 Dixieland, in jazz parlance
10 Missile with a target
14 Pal of Kukla or Stan
15 Plexus
16 Profess
17 BASSET
19 Proper
20 Cowboy "____ Tall Jones"
21 French king or Cardinals' home
23 Marshal at Waterloo
24 Broadway sound designer Munderloh
26 ____ Lingus
27 Reverend in India
29 HOT SCAM
35 Fat Albert's friend
38 Date
39 It may be square
40 Not really fat
43 Appended
45 Schifrin in Hollywood music
46 Good Feeling was one
48 Wagons
49 IF FRESCO
53 Abner or Kim
54 United parent
55 To be in Latin
59 Chum
62 ____ Life (1989 movie with Anita Morris)
65 "He ain't heavy, ____ my brother"
66 Away from the wind
68 SLOW ELF
70 "Cry havoc and let slip the ____ of war!": Julius Caesar
71 Palpate
72 Charity organization, often
73 Message on a red octagon
74 Cab or bus follower
75 Rear

DOWN

1 Kind of manual
2 Murder in the Cathedral man
3 Mete out
4 Unburden
5 Girls coming out
6 Irish vale famous for its Rose
7 Vacation destinations
8 Site of only World War II battle on American soil
9 Stopped
10 Paterfamilias, familiarly
11 Bath water?
12 Descartes, for one
13 Low card
18 LGA postings
22 Sign of a happy angel?
25 Earth
28 Soak
30 Song from Michael Jackson's Thriller
31 Main
32 Musical work by Verdi or Elton John
33 Surfeit with sweetness
34 Layers of a sort
35 Centennial State, in old addresses
36 King of Norway or Denmark
37 Individual
41 Recites readily
42 Info on a timetable
44 Deg. for periodontist
47 Apart
50 The Company, for short
51 Stammer (arch.)
52 Elected, in Evian
56 Dazzled
57 Setting of The Third Man's climactic scene
58 Big Bertha's birthplace
59 Rocket sites
60 Quite a bit
61 Toy that means "play well" in Danish
63 "What's the big ____ ?"
64 They're usually hon.
67 Sixth sense, for short
69 Man whose wife was hardened?

LETTER PERFECT

CROSSWORD PUZZLE NUMBER FOUR

ACROSS

1 Crenshaw's cousin
7 Digital alternative
13 Conscienceless
14 Adjective for Prince Albert II of Monaco
15 This puzzle's theme, exemplified in 1, 14, 30, 42, 62, and 65 across and 16 down
16 Believer in kismet
18 Double curve
19 Native of Muscat
21 Detective Fin Tutuola on *Law & Order: Special Victims Unit*
22 Put things back in the suitcase
24 Sono of the Ballet Russe
25 *Lend* _____ (1948 Broadway revue)
28 Lime in *The Third Man*
30 Sponge Bob's Bottom
32 Eye drop
33 Lamb's dam
36 Pre-owned
37 Word with tin or tune
39 Flaherty's *Man of* _____
40 McCourt book
41 It may be on a roll
42 Ornate style
44 Pave the way (to)
46 Currency in Cuernavaca
47 Dangerous companion
50 Specks of land in the sea
52 Like Kerouac's generation
53 Mme. de Staël's was famous
54 JFK predecessor
57 With dexterity
59 Congenital
62 New Hampshire political family name
63 More expensive
64 Left
65 Orbital point of conjunction or opposition

DOWN

1 Capitulate, informally
2 Famous baker
3 Ms. Piggies
4 Is, for more than one
5 Florida's _____ Harbour
6 Journalist Joseph or Stewart
7 Vino area
8 Govt. arts funder
9 Robert Wuhl TV title role
10 Nikon rival
11 Start
12 Reach
16 With levity
17 Joint ornament
20 Gullet
22 Blitz
23 European sea eagle
24 It's over, in poetry
25 Neighbor
26 Type of decree
27 Pieces together, with "out"
29 Theatre critic John
31 Cuba or Puerto Rico, e.g.
33 Desire
34 Home of Texas Sports Hall of Fame
35 Adam's grandson
38 Centric
39 Experts
41 Brit. ref. bk.
43 Decide
44 Release
45 Org. including Fatah
47 Humble
48 *Apocalypse Now* _____ (recut version)
49 Nixon who sang for Audrey and Natalie
51 Bagnold and Blyton
53 Formal accessory
54 Fishing boat
55 Remnant
56 "_____ 'iggins, just you wait!"
58 Saturn or opal finish
60 Napoleonic marshal
61 Luhrmann of *Moulin Rouge!*

MINDING PEAS AND CUES

CROSSWORD PUZZLE NUMBER FIVE

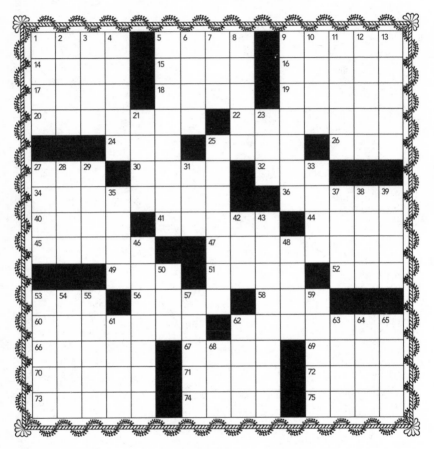

ACROSS

1 Cinch

5 Get by

9 Helvetian

14 Italian capital

15 Iris gets color from it

16 Holding

17 Some of them are orange

18 Kind of guard or admiral

19 Everything old new again

20 Cable network covering ocean's width?

22 Perfect offer from the optometrist?

24 Polish off

25 Horizontal passage from the surface of a mine

26 Shepard's *A _____ of the Mind*

27 Miller's _____ *My Sons*

30 Counterpart to FDIC for brokerages

32 Ratio of a no. to 100

34 Second-rate film with actress Arthur?

36 They are guests on "Saturday Night Live"

40 Van Druten's _____ *Camera*

41 Legal bar

44 Final Four initials

45 Cheeses from Holland

47 Be in debt to boyfriends for wind instruments?

49 Likely

51 Philly Pops conductor

52 66, e.g.

53 Word preceding sis-boom-bah

56 Seine feeder

58 Brother

60 German sheep ship?

62 Instructions for cleaning billiard equipment with cotton swabs?

66 Charmer or alarmer

67 Auteur Egoyan

69 First word in name of a Tulsa university

70 Jagged

71 Sped

72 _____ Flynn Boyle

73 Domingo, for one

74 Simply ages

75 Frogs do it

DOWN

1 Watery heptad

2 Coward's _____ *with Violin*

3 Length times width

4 Group usually pursuing outlaws

5 Salutary

6 Kiln

7 Nuisance to a certain princess

8 Like some seals

9 Time in stir

10 Garden pest

11 Chip maker

12 Caravansary

13 Sacerdotal symbol

21 El _____

23 Harburg the lyricist, to his pals

25 Flammable solvent

27 Rose's lover in a long-running Broadway play

28 Clue, maybe

29 Nash's one-L priest

31 Magnum and others

33 What to wait for before speaking sometimes

35 Van Druten's *I Remember _____*

37 Blemish

38 High-strung

39 Poet who wrote "Six Blind Men and the Elephant"

42 IOU part

43 My Sin and Poison

46 One credited with saying "You have hissed my mystery lectures"

48 Word often preceded by crashing

50 Carrere or Texada of films

53 Button on a pedometer

54 *Bird on _____* (1990 Goldie Hawn-Mel Gibson film)

55 Wading bird

57 Washington, but not Adams or Jefferson

59 Bikini, for example

61 "Por un _____" (Gloria Estefan song)

62 Word with flower or flour

63 Dies _____ (Day of wrath in a hymn)

64 Medic or legal prefix

65 Insult

68 Unduly

NO END IN SIGHT

CROSSWORD PUZZLE NUMBER SIX

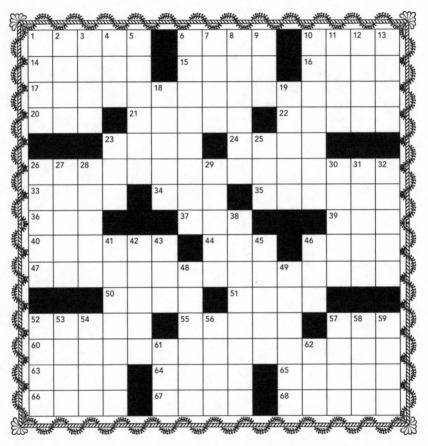

ACROSS

1 Like Mount Everest and the Gobi Desert

6 National Geographic Society products

10 It's pretty thick

14 Memorable Waikiki entertainer

15 Rapper-actor whose name sounds like a drink

16 King Diarmuid's capital

17 Popular name of Schubert work in B minor!

20 It may be inflated

21 Key on the right

22 Robert Burns's "_____ Wi' a Tocher"

23 Legatee

24 Container from which the word "tweezers" was derived

26 Merriam-Webster's Collegiate, for one!

33 "_____ Me" (Elton John/Bernie Taupin song)

34 Galley propellant

35 Rib

36 Ivanov of the Russian Imperial Ballet

37 Director Browning of *Dracula*

39 Cash extension

40 "Both a blessing and _____"

44 With 45-Down, Neapolitan song on which "It's Now or Never" is based

46 Dog breed from Flanders, for short

47 Surfing movie of 1966!

50 Big bank, familiarly

51 Young kangaroo

52 More than evidence

55 Chameleon, for one

57 Subj. with equations

60 Reason a check might not be honored!

63 Feeler

64 Occupies a base

65 Aquarium brightener

66 Those in Mexico

67 Kind of boy on a film crew

68 Beginning

DOWN

1 Previn's together

2 Small amount, perhaps

3 The skinny

4 Tuna for sushi

5 "You can forget about it"

6 Abuse

7 Problem for the head or the heart

8 Looked closely

9 Sem. deg.

10 Ascetic who lived atop a pillar

11 Panchen _____

12 Certain Dadaist sculptures

13 Putdowns from Scrooge

18 Jones who designed the Queen's House at Greenwich

19 Béarnaise or Bordelaise, for example

23 Kept out of sight

25 Gift for a tenth wedding anniversary

26 G-sharp's twin

27 Wood mentioned in a beer commercial

28 Ziegfeld Follies, for one

29 Suffix denoting a running course

30 "Sawing logs," for example

31 Oily corrosive solution

32 Chutzpah

38 Separate

41 Makes up for

42 Express disdain, in a way

43 Spring forward to this in NYC

45 See 44-Across

46 Believe

48 Establish a connection

49 Taken care of

52 Kind of organ

53 Cellular controllers

54 Norwegian city in Czechoslovakia?

56 Sgts. and cpls.

57 PM's

58 Jig or wobbler

59 Something to strain at

61 Little white lie

62 The first ever in Olympic gymnastics was in 1976

SURPRISE ENDINGS

CROSSWORD PUZZLE NUMBER SEVEN

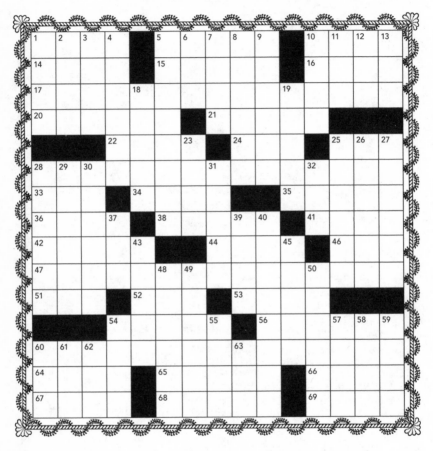

ACROSS

1 It includes asana and pranayama
5 Caesar or Cobb
10 Followed
14 Bohemian, for one
15 Linen
16 "Home is heaven and orgies are _____": Ogden Nash
17 "The Raven" and "Annabel Lee," for example?
20 Political writer known as "Scotty"
21 Cause of some tears
22 Quattro maker
24 Head Start and Job Corps agcy.
25 Words before carte
28 What *Rose et Blanche* and *Elle et lui* were written on?
33 Kind of cake or meal
34 Tiller
35 Exhausted
36 Plaintiff Scott in 1857 Supreme Court case
38 Pews and park benches
41 "Answer yes _____"
42 Young nocturnal bird
44 Three- _____ sloth
46 Year in Trajan's reign
47 Young women's roles in *Picnic* or *Bus Stop*?
51 OXFAM or CARE, e.g.
52 One of Knute's successors
53 Supporting role in *Peter Pan*
54 Crossword puzzle forms
56 Rubs out
60 Distinctive style of *The Magic Mountain* or *Buddenbrooks*?
64 Singer from Ibadan
65 Patronize, as a restaurant
66 *Sesame Street* Muppet
67 Place west of Nod
68 Social climbers
69 Film director Nicolas

DOWN

1 World War I battles were fought about it
2 It's often within Ye Shoppe
3 Letterman and Leno material
4 Divine incarnation
5 Straphangers, maybe
6 "You've got mail" company
7 Stitch companion
8 Support group in more than 100 countries
9 Turned down
10 Kind of lady who calls?
11 Easy simile
12 Street in horror films
13 Broadway's McAnuff
18 Kind of rider in the Spanish-American War
19 Puts out of breath
23 Man, for one
25 Precis
26 *Of Mice and Men* character
27 French region noted for water wells
28 "_____, Moses" (spiritual)
29 Harmless insect
30 Opera by Verdi or Rossini
31 Stradivarius alternative
32 Soldier's address
37 San Diego's _____ Coronado Hotel
39 A lot
40 Parts
43 Coronet
45 Plow man
48 Gets up
49 Norman Bates, for one
50 Closer
54 James Cagney action film
55 First Asian winner of Nobel Peace Prize (1974)
57 Granary
58 Girl's name in a Salinger title
59 Big city miasma
60 Monogram of "Four Quartets" poet
61 Tricked
62 Keats's "To Autumn," e.g.
63 Collar

WINNING WORDS

CROSSWORD PUZZLE NUMBER EIGHT

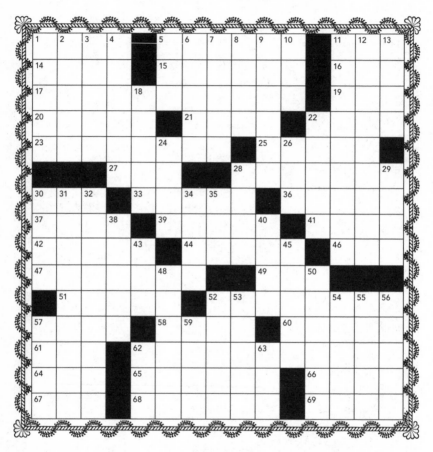

ACROSS

1 Promenade

5 Injury

11 Type of camera first made in 1935: abbr.

14 Hit, perhaps, by a Met player

15 Auto safety device

16 Bluegrass

17 *Replacement

19 _____ and Ray, authors of popular political science textbook

20 Late news?

21 Time for a pol or a con

22 Baseball family whose real name is Rojas

23 With 52 Across and 35 Down, where answers to clues marked with * were winning words

25 Group that lived in Asgard

27 Stat. From U.S. Dept. of Labor

28 European cavalry

30 Oscar winner for *Cimarron*

33 Diver's equipment

36 Turning tool

37 Balin and Claire

39 Standing tall

41 No idler

42 Bunsen alternatives

44 Theatrical lights

46 Churchill's "so few"

47 Bird dogs

49 Constricting scarf?

51 June moon, for example

52 See 23 Across

57 "Are you ____ out?"

58 "That was a silly thing to do!"

60 An unspoken language

61 Sequel to *Angela's Ashes*

62 *Nonchalant

64 DiFranco of Righteous Babe Records

65 Soprano called "La Divina"

66 Scurries

67 Certain linemen, for short

68 They can be caused by ink or blood

69 Unpleasant sound for a bicyclist or an actor

DOWN

1 Mozart or Sousa, for example

2 Island of which Oranjestad is the Capital

3 Conforming to regulations

4 Kind of acid used in skin cosmetics

5 Shaveling

6 Synonym and near-anagram of "lariat"

7 Synthetic fiber last manufactured in 1986

8 Adjective for Nietzsche's "mensch"

9 Movement in Kenya in the 1950s

10 SAM's counterpart

11 *Marauder

12 *Excessive verbosity

13 Prego rival

18 Acronym for programs in which workers gain corporate shares

22 Important name in Syria

24 Home of the Promenade des Anglais

26 Subj. often taught in night school

28 Grub Street denizen

29 Esne, perhaps

30 First chairman of the House Un-American Activities Committee

31 *One way to learn the ropes

32 *Strawberry plant disease causing yellow leaves

34 Modern addresses

35 See 23 across

38 Dionysian reveler

40 First words of notable Hamlet soliloquy

43 Where a D.D. may be awarded

45 Kind of power

48 Paint again

50 ____ Law (Sharia)

52 Short vodka?

53 Louisiana praline ingredient

54 "____ fatuus" (deceptive goal)

55 Dostoyevsky's ____ *from the Underground*

56 Cagney on TV

57 Acronym before TASS

59 Carol Burnett's alma mater

62 Dells, e.g.

63 Naval ship letters

WORD PLACEMENT

CROSSWORD PUZZLE NUMBER NINE

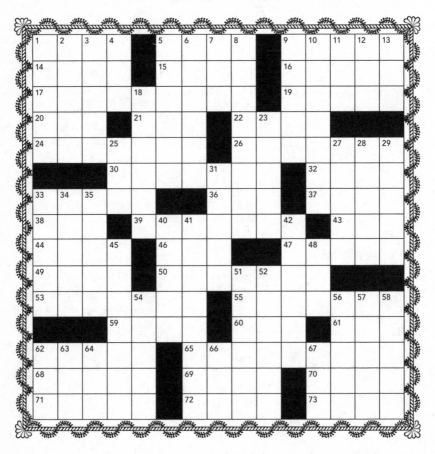

ACROSS

1 Master
5 Shindig
9 Acetate or phosphate
14 Suffix indicating adherents
15 James of the blues
16 String section
17 With 20 across, irate!
19 Uncanny
20 See 17 across
21 Ms. Farrow
22 Cubs' groups
24 Early ascetics
26 Claim of some sweeteners!
30 Trendy restaurants
32 Profess
33 Nickname of noted French architect
36 Ox tail?
37 Beget
38 _____ roll
39 Situation comedy from 2000 to 2006 on Fox network!
43 Immoderately
44 JDs or LLBs
46 Tic-toe connection
47 Where the Minutemen play, informally
49 Ordinary
50 Pettifog
53 Common lumber size!
55 Poem by Poe
59 Sir Herbert Beerbohm _____
60 Genetic matl.
61 With 65 Across, conclude optimistically!
62 Winner of 1961 Best Actress Oscar
65 See 61 Across
68 Maine's main college town
69 Franchot of stage and screen
70 Pizza producer
71 Middle
72 It may be cutting
73 Old letter opener

DOWN

1 Give one-tenth
2 One of the Three Musketeers
3 Encounters
4 Computer key
5 Contradicts
6 Song associated with 15 Across
7 Where the RR stops
8 Difficult
9 Ties
10 Afternoon rests
11 Craggy hill
12 Yalie
13 _____ Dawn Chong
18 _____ -gatherum
23 Support for oils
25 Half of *Chicago* songwriting team
27 Musical set in Argentina
28 Peter and the Wolfe?
29 Sweet round treats
31 Christina who starred in "The Addams Family"
33 It may be clear
34 Sign on disabled vehicles
35 Oscar-nominated Hoffman role
40 "Ave _____ Vale" (poem by Catullus)
41 Honored poet
42 Muslim teacher
45 Impairs resistance
48 _____ culpa
51 Danish navigator for whom a North Pacific sea is named
52 Elastic cord
54 "Here I come, ready _____ !"
56 Tenth-century pope
57 Lay away
58 Barbara and Anthony
62 Moo
63 _____ pro nobis
64 Louis or Charles, par exemple
66 Brick trough
67 Tel. and S.S., e.g.

X-RATED

CROSSWORD PUZZLE NUMBER TEN

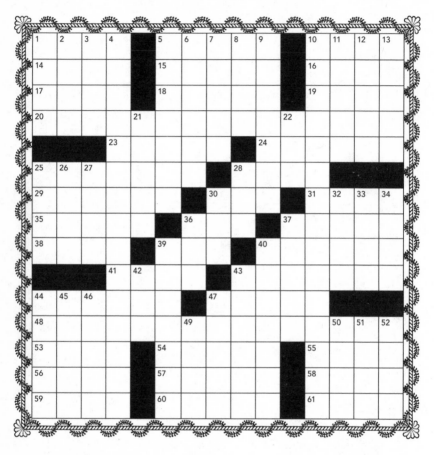

ACROSS

1 The "bad" in "my bad"

5 Does what a director or a fisherman may do

10 Ingredient of a Greek salad

14 Where Bill the Goat first appeared in 1893 (Abbr.)

15 Egg producer

16 Filmdom's Lena or Ken

17 River of Hades

18 Nixon's TV producer

19 Gabrielle's warrior companion

94

20 Spell, Roman law, Mae West play, spicy cuisine

23 Principle

24 Plaza denizen in books

25 Failing to RSVP, say

28 The big picture

29 Cioppino ingredient

30 Really big sizes

31 Mrs. Dithers in "Blondie"

35 "This Was ____ Nice Clambake" (song from Carousel)

36 A Rose in "Guns N' Roses"

37 Stanley or Helen on "Three's Company"

38 Gummo, for one

39 Old-fashioned tel. switchboard

40 An Andrews Sister

41 34 Down in Rome

43 Beverly Sills's nickname

44 Suit

47 Perez Prado dance music

48 French city, women's suffrage Amendment, jazzman Beiderbecke, cowboy Tom, pickle

53 The final word?

54 Mad as a hornet

55 Frilly

56 Rochon of Waiting to Exhale

57 Consumer

58 First battleship in the Russian Navy

59 Holly

60 Battle signs

61 Greek combining form meaning dry

DOWN

1 Overdo it in conversation

2 Greek combining form meaning bone

3 Chalcedony

4 Office machine, lenient, inventor Adolphe, surrealist Ernst, April duty

5 Kind of cable

6 Dispatch boats

7 Home of the House of Seven Gables

8 Sci. museum feature, often

9 Functional units

10 18 Across's news group, losing tic-tac-toe line, actor Brian, kind of hedge, some salmon

11 Oleoresin

12 Flatware parts

13 "Lizzie Borden took ____ . . ."

21 Kick out

22 Guido's musical syllable

25 Kind of radio

26 Nimbus

27 Kind of ID

28 Kind of wind in a saying

30 Vin Diesel movie and 3 of 23 in this puzzle

32 Astra producer

33 Auberjonois or Descartes

34 41 Across in Greece

36 Pecs' and delts' cousins

37 Ben Ezra, for one

39 Head honchos

40 New Year's Day paraders in Philadelphia

42 Faulkner's ___ Lay Dying

43 Bandleader Les of "Quiet Village"

44 Site of Revolutionary War massacre in Pennsylvania

45 Subject of "Marquis of Queensbury vs. Oscar Wilde"

46 Punishment for Napoleon and Trotsky

47 Sporty Mazda

49 Bric-a- ____

50 Advance

51 Confectioner, at times

52 Phone connection?

CHAPTER FIVE

IF YOU SAY SO

Wellerisms, Tom Swifties, Croakers, and Envelope-Pushers

"I was on John Kerry's boat,"
said Tom swiftly.

Sam Weller is Mr. Pickwick's cheeky valet in Charles Dickens's *The Pickwick Papers*. On occasion he expresses himself in a punning fashion by putting a literal interpretation on a metaphorical idiom and following it with a facetious comparison: This type of witticism was known in the nineteenth century as a "Wellerism."

"[O]ut with it, as the father said to the child, ven he swallowed a farden [farthing]"
and
"Wery glad to see you indeed; and hope our acquaintance may be a long 'un, as the gen'lm'n said to the fi' pun' note."

Of more recent vintage is this example that might qualify:

"We'll have to rehearse it," as the undertaker said when the coffin fell from the funeral car.

Humorous forms never stand still, and Wellerisms developed in the early twentieth century into what are known as "Tom Swifties." Tom Swift is the intrepid young hero of a series of boys' books, the first of which, *Tom Swift and His Motor-Cycle*, was published in 1910. (The publisher, Edward Stratemeyer, was also responsible for creating the Bobbsey Twins, Hardy Boys, Rover Boys, Uncle Wiggly, and Don Sturdy books.) The style in the Tom Swift books became noted, not altogether justly, for repeated use of various adverbs to modify the phrase "Tom said." Some actual examples from the early books include:

* "'The man lost this from his pocket, Dad,' said Tom eagerly."
* "'You've missed it!' said Tom grimly as the machine started."
* "'I wouldn't call a constable,' said Tom, quietly."

In reality, Tom's chum, Ned Newton, is much more apt to have his sayings modified with an awkward adverb, as in:

* "'This went mostly backward—in my direction,' said Ned ruefully."
* "'The recoil?' questioned Ned, wonderingly."
* "'What have you got it painted red for?' Ned asked pantingly."

Pantingly? Okay, if you say so, Ned. In any event, a type of pun using the name of Tom Swift accompanied by an adverb relating, often preposterously, to what Tom was saying, became quite popular from the 1920s onward. Here are a few hot-off-the-press examples, your author said exemplarily:

* "All my employees are on strike," Tom said helplessly.
* "My radio works perfectly now," Tom said ecstatically.
* "Sharpen this pencil," Tom said bluntly.
* "Thanks for sharpening it," Tom said pointedly.
* "Is it Gothic or Romanesque?" Tom asked archly.
* "That hurts!" Tom said smartly.

"This stew needs more flavor," Tom said sagely.
"I'll add some of this bitter herb," Tom said ruefully.
"Maybe another herb would be better," Tom said thymely.
"And a dash or two of this one," Tom said as he rose merrily.

---

* "I like both apple and plum," Tom said tartly.
* "What sort is it?" Tom asked kindly.
* "I'll have a 12-to-1 Martini," Tom said dryly.
* "I've just read Sophocles's *Eumenides*," Tom said furiously.
* "Which way to Calvary?" Tom asked crossly.
* "That's a lot of hay," Tom said balefully.
* "I loved *Shrek*," Tom said animatedly.
* "I'll have a bowl of Chinese soup," Tom said wantonly.
* "I have a perfect driving record," Tom said recklessly.
* "I'll try again to learn this code," Tom said remorsefully.
* "I subscribe to several magazines," Tom said periodically.
* "Where are all the daunts?" Tom said dauntlessly.
* "Bah," Tom said sheepishly.

Well, it does tend to get out of hand. The Web site fun-with-words.com is among many that offer hundreds of often exquisitely witty examples of the form. Three of your author's favorites from that site are:

* "I haven't had any tooth decay yet," said Tom precariously.
* "Your honor, you're crazy," said Tom judgmentally.
* "Elvis is dead," said Tom expressly.

Variants on the adverbial Tom Swifty include those that are adjectival, rather than adverbial, and name an appropriate speaker other than Tom, such as these examples devised by the author:

* "I am not interested," said the bank manager.
* "I've been discharged," said the electrician.
* "I am disconsolate," said the ex-diplomat.
* "I am depressed," said the former journalist.
* "I am repressed," said the journalist when he was rehired.
* "I am compressed," said the online journalist.
* "I am distressed," said the bald man.
* "I am elated," said the tardy techie.
* "I am stumped," said the lumberjack.
* "You are mistaken," said the kidnapper to his captive when he realized he had abducted the wrong child.

"I'm afraid I'm unbearable," said the childless woman.
"No," said her husband. "You're impregnable."
"Perhaps," said the wife, "it is you who are inconceivable."

Yet another variant, known as the "croaker," uses verbs instead of adverbs or adjectives to make its punning point. The croaker, says Willard Espy in *Almanac of Words at Play*, was invented by the writer Roy Bongartz in the pages of the *Saturday Review*. It is so called because of Bongartz's signature invention: "'I'm dying,' he croaked." Here are a few of the author's croakers that suggest you'd

better be careful about what you allow to
rattle around in your mind:

* "It should be 'whom' not
  'who,'" the grammarian
  objected.
* "I have to sweep up now," the
  custodian maintained.
* "This paper deserves a C, not a B,"
  the professor remarked.
* "I think Puerto Rico should be No. 51," the politician stated.
* "I'll dock the ship again," the captain reported.
* "Here's where I do my online elocution experiments," the
  speech teacher elaborated.
* "Shall I take the soprano or the alto part?" the singer
  inquired.
* "Here's where I'll put the kitchen, the den, and the parlor,"
  the architect ruminated.
* "You owe more tax," the IRS agent recollected.
* "I'll try that number again," the operator recalled.
* "Glaciers have created mountains where it used to be flat,"
  the geologist explained.
* "Here are my dues for next year," the club member
  rejoined.
* "Give me a thicker piece of wood," the carpenter replied.
* "We don't want to be another Florida," the election official
  recounted.
* "This is the second time you've been tardy," the teacher
  related.
* "This is my new mink coat," the socialite inferred.

* "I work in the prison cocktail lounge," the barman contended.

———◆———

Yet another Tom Swifty variant is known by your author as the "envelope-pusher." Its basis is to fashion an idiom or metaphor into a participial phrase followed by a sentence that, like the Wellerism mentioned earlier, takes the idiom literally or with a meaning other than the one intended. The name "envelope-pusher" comes from this flagship example:

* Pushing the envelope, the postman squeezed it through the narrow mail slot.
  Gluttons for this kind of punishment will read further to encounter more of the author's envelope-pushing concoctions.
* Striking a happy medium, the customer slapped the smiling spiritualist.
* Taking his *Time*, the reader removed the magazine from the rack.
* Hiding his pride, the zookeeper put the lions in a remote place.
* Hitting the road, the workmen created a large pothole.
* Sticking to his guns, the hunter wished he hadn't put his fingers in the superglue.
* Thinking outside the box, the philosopher wondered why he had crawled into the packing case in the first place.
* Casing the joint, the burglar placed the marijuana cigarette in a box.
* Stopping at nothing, the traveler found himself in a huge void.
* Bending the rules, the draftsman found the plastic ones easier to work with than the wooden ones.

* Beating around the bush, the gardener packed the soil down firmly.

* Unable to cut the mustard, the diner put mayonnaise on his sandwich.

* Drinking like a fish, the ichthyologist found the aquarium water was not very tasty.

* Foaming at the mouth, the early riser realized he had used too much toothpaste.

* Getting down to brass tacks, the carpenter wished he had brought more nails.

* Hitting the books, the student damaged the covers of the Dickens and the Dostoevsky novels.

* Keeping an eye on the table, the ocularist worked on the prosthesis.

* Calling a spade a spade, the poker player laid down a straight flush.

* Turning the tables on their opponents, the bridge players made dummies of themselves.

* Busting his chops, the chef made hamburger meat.

* Letting the cat out of the bag and spilling the beans, the pet lover provided a feast for his tabby.

* Talking through his hat, the announcer was very hard to understand.

* Making a long story short, the editor deleted every other paragraph.

That last one is not to be taken to heart by the editor or by readers of this modest volume, no matter how tempted they may be.

CHAPTER SIX

BEWARE THE DOGGEREL!

Rhymes Without Reason

I fear you'll find I'm just an amateur
At writing iambic pentameter.
And there's no doubt that you will think my trochee
Is much too lackluster and very low-key.
Spondaic, anapestic, or dactylic—
My verses never seem to be idyllic.
But I don't moan or groan, complain or curse,
For while my rhymes are bad, they could be verse.

—Your author

Russell Baker, that roguish wit with two Pulitzer Prizes on his nightstand, introduces *The Norton Book of Light Verse* with a reference to the "childish love of verse" that "comes bursting now and then out of prose-calloused adults in the most improbable settings, sometimes with macabre results." All right, all you prose-calloused readers, throw off those chains of expository, narrative, and descriptive writing, and wallow a bit in a bubble bath of rhyme, meter, and (mostly) nonsense. As for the macabre, well, if you're looking for it, you'll nearly always find it lurking somewhere.

These bits of doggerel, a word that Webster defines as "loose or irregular verse" (perhaps milk of magnesia is called for) or verse that is "burlesque, comic, mean, undignified, and trivial" (well, ex*cuse* me!), are the work of your author unless otherwise noted, and have been arranged more or less according to the subjects they deal with. Love being the most popular topic of the classic bards, it seems appropriate to begin with some verses in praise (or not) of romance.

ISLAND LOVE SONG

Let's meet in the moonlight in the Galápagos,
It's a place where neither your mama nor papa goes.
We'll find a nice spot to show our affection
And test Darwin's theory of natural selection.

THIRD-DEGREE BURNS

My love is like a red, red rose,
Much nicer than a spiny cactus.
I thought 'twas true love, I suppose,
Until your friend showed up and whacked us.

VALENTINE POEM

Most roses I have seen are bright, bright red,
But some of them are yellow.
To rhyme, you cannot be a girl—instead
You'd have to be a fellow.

WISHFUL THINKING

Until I met you, I was lonely,
Then we made love, and I at last
Believed I had achieved orgasm.
But now I think that it was only

Some stomach gas that I had passed
Resulting in a gastric spasm.

MY HEART LEAPS UP FOR LEPIDOPTERA
I used to think you were a butterfly
As you would flit and float from flower to flower.
But now each time I see you flutter by,
You make me think of Mamie Eisenhower

ICH-THEOLOGY
An amorous prawn and a sexy young scallop
Made love in a quaint old aquarium.
Their passion was great and they went at full gallop
In search of a monkfish who'd marry 'em.

But all the best planning of mice, men, and fish,
Alas, can go badly astray,
And the scallop wound up in nice pasta dish
And the prawn in a fine étouffée.

TO LUCY
(*Australopithecus afarensis*, a 3.2 million-year-old fossil)
Oh, Lucy, you're the one that I adore,
For you I have a lusty yen.
But, Lucy, I am only sixty-four,
And you won't see three million again.

In the same scientific vein, here is a complicated verse that will be
enhanced for the romantic reader who possesses some knowledge of
biological terms (no, not that kind, the scientific kind you'll find in
science museums). The poet this time is not your author, but his son,

Paul. It just shows that a tendency to wax poetic must be a mania that runs in the family.

DOPAMINE, EPINEPHRINE, VALENTINE
Roses are of wavelength (nanometers) six fifty;
Violets at four hundred are still pretty nifty.
Sucrose makes that T1R receptor jingle,
Just like you make
My little amygdala tingle.

Your lips, like a twin luscious gastropod pulmonate,
Just make me wanna grab you, get close, and osculate.
And I fantasize about your auricular pinnae;
They tickle my face
Like plumose antennae.

Your tresses scintillate like some glimmering parhelia,
Obsessing my heart with a simmering trichophilia.
Your ocular orbs are like dark ferrohornblende;
Your curvaceous philtrum
Could start a new porn trend.

Your body is hot—just like a sublime teen;
Your mind fascinates like a *CSI* crime scene.
Your jokes are too funny; your gossip, too juicy;
Your movements are graceful, just like that ape Lucy.
The mere glimpse of you can bring me to climax;
You're ten times the thrill
Of a full 3D IMAX®.

It's hard to define loves like our own
(But you know 'em when you see 'em).

In time, our deep passions have grown
(Much like this booming museum).
No bond in this world could match our alliance.
We'll just chalk it up to natural science!

—◆—

The animal kingdom has been the inspiration for such classic works as "The Gingham Dog and the Calico Cat," "Ode to a Nightingale," and "Jeremiah Was A Bullfrog," none of which appears in this volume. In their stead are a few more bits of fauna, these from the fevered brain of your author.

LITTLE-KNOWN FACT

The *Symbion pandora*
Has neither a knee nor a hip.
It's *fauna*, though, not *flora*
And lives on a lobster's lip.

MOOED INDIGO

Oh, once I saw a purple cow,
To see her made me grin.
But then I made a solemn vow
That I would lay off gin.

GOOD BREEDING

With a proud Siamese
I am never at ease,
And a lofty Burmese
Makes me sniffle and sneeze.
True, I take a dim view
Of a grim Russian Blue,
And a poor tailless Manx,
Gets my "Thanks, but no thanks."

I can't hide my aversion
To a fluffy-haired Persian.
And I really can't bear
A Domestic Short Hair
Or a smug Abyssinian—
At least that's my opinion.
But there's one kind of feline
To whom I make a beeline
And with whom I will dally:
That's the breed known as Alley.

DOWN, BOY

He's man's best friend, or so they say,
But I think a dog is a danger
Who is eager to lunge at my throat.
No, man's best friend can stay away,
I'd rather that he'd be a stranger.
For a pet, just give me a goat.

ONE LIFE TO LIVE

A tomcat I once knew
Was amorous—and daring.
His life of derring-do
Was dangerous—and wearing.
He did not have nine lives,
Oh, no, his days were few,
But, oh!—he had nine wives
And countless rendezvous.

—◆—

Getting along in years has inspired many a poet among old codgers, a category that includes your author. Ah, those golden senior moments!

REMEMBRANCE OF THINGS PAST
It's true I've not started to wheeze or to creak yet,
And those sexy ads for Victoria's Secret
Can sure tantalize me—oh yes, how they titillate!
It's too bad at my age it's all just a little late.

LOOKING FORWARD
"Grow old," Ben Ezra said, "the best
Is yet to be." But did he jest?
What is to be, young whippersnappers,
Are items sent in plain brown wrappers,
Like paltry pills and useless unctions
To combat sexual dysfunctions.

TRANSIENT DENTALISM
The teeth decay, the teeth decay—that's fate,
And after many an inlay comes the plate.

MEMENTO MORI
As gray hairs grow upon your head, you'll
Find more funerals in your schedule.
One happy thought all grief obscures:
At least, this funeral isn't yours.

CONSOLATION
As more friends go to meet their Maker,
It benefits the undertaker,
And though I feel profound distress—
Each year my gift list costs me less.

Travel, food, and wine—now those are topics that could bring out
the poetry in anyone.

LIKE THE MAN SAID . . .

I never would cavil
Or carp with Bob Benchley.
American travel,
He once said, essentially
Has only two classes.
Find that bewilderin'?
The truth still, alas, is:
First-class and with children.

EASY CHOICE

I prefer something chocolaty
To anything broccolity.

IT'S ALL IN THE PACKAGING

Celery comes in stalks,
Asparagus in spears.
Grapes are in bunches
And sweet corn in ears.
Cheese comes in wedges,
Champagne is in splits.
But saltine crackers
Always come in bits.

PLAYING CATCH-UP

(*after Ogden Nash and Richard Armour*)
The ketchup in that shaken bottle
Spews forth as through a funnel.
And while it may be true a lot'll
Come—eventually, none'll.

The office is where many people spend a great deal of their time. And as the British and American versions of *The Office* attempt to show us, and as Dilbert and real life consistently prove, there's comedy in them thar cubicles. Here's some (it is hoped).

CRASH COURSE

My hard disk has crashed
For reasons inscrutable.
My teeth are all gnashed,
My work's uncomputable.
Some wires must be crossed
And I'm going to crack up,
My files are all lost,
I don't have a backup.
Despair's absolute,
All efforts are fruitless.
I try to reboot,
Attempts are quite bootless.
The fault, I feel sure:
A dreadful new virus
For which there's no cure.
So now what? Papyrus?

LET'S COMMUNICATE

Our office intercom is strange
And seems to have too short a range.
Each time I try to contact you,
I'm never able to get through.
But you can clearly hear me call
If I just holler down the hall.

MIS-LEAD

Behold the handiest of all utensils—
An electric sharpener for pencils.
But when at last its work is finished
The pencil's size is so diminished
I think
I can
Discern
The point
Of no
Return.

LOTS OF PARKING

In our company parking lot
A number's put on every slot.
The first is closest to the door,
The last—halfway to Singapore.
And to be sure that things are fair,
We have a plan for who parks where.

The spaces are assigned by lot,
As drawn from names placed in a pot.
But I'm aware, since I'm no fool,
There are exceptions to this rule:
The Boss, of course, gets Number One,
And Number Two is for his son.
The third slot goes to old Sam Lane,
Who's just begun to use a cane.
Four female workers get the next,
So by no muggers they'll be vexed.
Our I.T. whiz has Number Eight
Because he always works so late.

Of parking spots, we have a lot,
But I don't think our plan's so hot—
Since everyone's a special case,
Entitled to a premium space,
And so it goes, on down the line,
Right to the last slot—that one's mine.

TIME OUT

Our office clock leaves me aghast,
It isn't right, I know.
At 8 A.M. it's always fast.
By 5 P.M., it's slow.

AUTOMATED TELEPHONE ANSWERING SYSTEM

"Thanks for calling: now before you speak,
Please notice that this menu changed last week.
So if you know the number of the line
You want, press '1' and then the '#' sign.
This activates the direct-dialing mode,
Then you can dial the seven-digit code.
If you just know your party's name, you'd better
Press a '2' and then the name's first letter.
You'll be directed by a voice command
To quickly press the next two letters, and
Your call will be connected right away.
To hear this message once again, just say
In English, very slow, "Reiterate."
Then when you hear the ring-tone, press the '8.'
If you're unsure of what you want, then you
Must press the '*' to hear a new 'Menu.'
If all else fails and you need help, why then

Press '5' and then the '#' sign again,
When prompted, you should just say 'Yes' or 'No'—"
Oh, never mind, I hung up long ago.

OFFICE PARTY

Our conference room is all festooned
With strands of red crepe paper,
A piano has arrived (untuned),
We're set to prance and caper.

Come one, come all, to drink and eat,
Enjoy a laugh that's hearty.
The boss provides this yearly treat,
The dreaded Christmas party.
The boss decides to tell a joke,
You know what's coming after.
Although his jokes can make you choke,
The room erupts in laughter.

The boss decides he'll tell one more,
So all remain attentive—
They've heard it thirty times before:
Their paycheck's their incentive.

Now Vera downs a glass of punch
And makes a pass at Benny.
It's too bad that she skipped her lunch,
'Cause she's had one too many.
And Benny doesn't even blink
(Sometimes he's so contrary),
So Vera takes another drink
And makes a pass at Mary.

Old Bill and Eddie are engaged
In heated conversation,
And somehow Bill becomes enraged
(He missed his medication).
Then Bill calls Eddie several names
(At least three "sons of bitches"),
And after all the fun and games,
Bill needs a dozen stitches.

Then dark and somber grows the mood,
Our minds are getting foggy.
Perhaps we'd better have some food:
The sandwiches are soggy,
The turkey's dry, the ham is fat,
The dips could not be thinner,
By now the champagne is all flat.
I wish I had some dinner.

At last the party's winding down,
Each worker and superior
Will tell you with a fearful frown
It could not have been drearier.
Why don't we cancel this event,
Rewrite the office manual?
But what the hey—let's be content
At least it's only annual.

THE RAISE

I'm neatly dressed,
My clothes are pressed,
Every hair's in place.
My nerves are calm,

I've great aplomb,
And elegance, and grace.

I stand before
The boss's door,
I'm confident, serene,
I've done my job,
I turn the knob,
It's my turn to be seen.

I say, "Good day,"
And make my way
Across the floor to where
I flash a smile
And then, with style,
Sit in the proffered chair.

With infinite
Finesse and wit
I smoothly have my say,
With steady nerve
Prove I deserve
A hefty raise in pay.

The boss agrees,
We're both at ease,
With confidence I leave.
The deed is done,
The raise I won
I'm happy to receive.

This slick technique
Is quick and sleek—

Or that's the way it seems,
For such success,
I must confess,
Is only in my dreams.

HARASSMENT POLICY

If a coworker's glances
Should lead on to advances,
And I can't decide what the pass meant,
If I went by the book,
After one ribald look,
I'd holler, "Ah ha! That's harássment!"

But I don't have the nerve
When I'm thrown such a curve,
For I fear I would suffer embarrassment,
If I started to shout,
And someone pointed out
That the pronunciation is "hárassment."

❧

In the same vein of puzzling pronunciations are these verses, called "Six States of Mind," which must be read carefully (if at all) in order to make any sense of them.

When it's dry in Bangor, ME,
Farmers there can feel the PE.
But they don't gripe or groan,
And they don't mope or moan,
They just kneel and pray for RE.

Folks down in Atlanta, GA
Fear the mad Lucrezia BA.

They'll all quickly say
You'd best run away
When you see her coming TA.

The oilmen down in Dallas, TX
All say, "There ain't a thing can VX.
We flourish and thrive
And all of us drive
A Rolls, a Cadillac, or LX."

Now when you visit Dover, DE,
Be very sure that you are WE
That a modest skirt
And a clean white shirt
Are what a well-dressed gal and FE.

The food in Detroit, MI,
Is great, and how I WI
To have some pastrami
With Polish salami—
I'd love that tasty DI.

A tenor in Wichita, KS
In each song sings all of the STS,
And has been known to gloat
That his very top note
Is much higher than Mario LS.

—◆—

Your author is grateful to Paul Bernhard for the next verse, which suitably concludes this chapter with a profound, if not exactly blithesome, insight about those who write such verses.

So many poems I have read,
I think I'm going to lose my head.
If I just look on one more verse,
I'll be inspired to curse . . . or worse.
Poems of people, poems of birds,
And poems filled with olde wordes.

I plow through stanzas, ceasing never.
Oh, wow! These guys can sure be clever!
Clever? Clever? They endeavor
To fill the world with needless rhyme
That takes up space and uses time.
Page on page of balderdash—
How could someone write such trash?

I do not know, nor do I care,
But look—the stuff is everywhere—
In dull old books with dusty pages
That haven't gotten looks for ages,
And bright new books with pages clean
That no one yet has even seen.
They're all just crazy, all just useless,
Just like hanging bad guys nooseless.

Now look what I have gone and done:
I've just made up another one
Just what we need—another poem,
Like carpets need someone to mow 'em.
Well, as they say (the ones who coin 'em),
If you can't beat those guys, then join 'em.
Seeing there's no use in fighting,
Poets will just keep on writing.

CHAPTER SEVEN

HAVE YOU TASTED YOUR WORM?

Spoonerisms, Malapropisms, Mondegreens, Eggcorns, and Holorimes

If the terriers and bariffs are torn down, this economy will grow.
—George W. Bush, January 7, 2000

You might think a "spooner" is a person who makes love in a silly, sentimental way, or possibly someone who manufactures spoons. The origin of the family name Spooner, however, is the Anglo-Saxon word *span*, meaning "chip" or "splinter," and it referred to someone who shingled roofs. The Reverend William Archibald Spooner, who was born in 1844 and died in 1930, was the Dean and Warden of New College, Oxford, and was not notable for spooning of any sort. Instead, he had the reputation of being prone to committing slips of the tongue in which he transposed the initial sounds of certain words: "right lane" instead of "light rain," for example. Such lapses became known as "spoonerisms," as a kind of tribute to the dizzy bean, er, busy dean. A spoonerism is often used synonymously with what extremely learned grammarians call "metathesis," which means the transposing of any elements in a language.

Although Spooner was the reputed speaker of dozens of funny sayings resulting from his supposed habit, most authoritative sources are reluctant to assert with authority that he did, in fact, say most of them. Bartlett's *Familiar Quotations* finds that "Kinquering Congs Their Titles Take" was indeed an actual utterance by Spooner in announcing the name of a hymn in college chapel. The *Oxford Dictionary of Quotations* allows one other as being out of Spooner's own mouth: "The weight of rages will press hard upon the employer."

Many others that are attributed to Spooner were probably concocted by some of his louche students or waggish colleagues. The most often quoted is Spooner's alleged admonition to a failing student: "You have hissed my mystery lectures, and were caught fighting a liar in the quad. Having tasted your worm, you will leave by the next town drain."

You can probably figure out what was presumably meant by that and by these other oft-quoted but unsubstantiated Spooner slips:

* "The Lord is a shoving leopard."
* "It is kisstomary to cuss the bride."
* "Mardon me, padam, this pie is occupewed. Can I sew you to another sheet?"
* "Let us glaze our asses to the queer old Dean."
* "We'll have the hags flung out."
* "It is important to have a well-boiled icicle."
* "He suffered a blushing crow."

The most frequent victims of accidental spoonerisms are probably radio and television announcers caught in the unpredictable excitement of covering live events. The hapless perpetrators of such bloopers are always inconsolably mortified, as announcers naturally tend to be when their mellifluousness is less than perfect. Famed radio announcer Harry Von Zell was known for having committed two thighslappers: "Here come the Duck and Doochess of Windsor" and "Ladies and gentlemen, the President of the United States, Hoobert Heever." When the renowned banjoist Eddie Peabody appeared on the National Barn Dance, the announcer blissfully told his audience, "And now, Eddie Playbody will pee for you." A British announcer once reported that a dignitary had been honored with a "twenty-one son galoot." A Canadian proudly intoned that he was speaking on the "Canadian Broadcorping Castration." In a report from Cap-Haïtien, Haiti, a French newsman spoke of "*les copulations immenses du Pape*" ("the immense copulations of the Pope") instead of "*les populations immenses du Cap*" ("the immense populations of the Cape.")

Most spoonerisms are purposely devised as jokes. W. C. Fields was the putative author of "I'd rather have a bottle in front of me than a frontal lobotomy," which was improved upon by Dean Martin's version: "I'd rather have a free bottle in front of me than a pre-frontal lobotomy." When George S. Kaufman's daughter told him that a friend had withdrawn from her classes at Vassar in order to get married, Kaufman spoonerized, "Ah, she put the heart before the course." At the University of California, Berkeley, a shuttle bus that takes students to the nearby stop of the Bay Area Rapid Transit is affectionately known as "Humphrey Go-BART." And then, of course, we must not overlook the albums by at least two rock bands, Metallica and Caravan, which are naughtily titled "Cunning Stunts."

The author's favorite manufactured spoonerism concerns a little girl named Shelly who was attending a wedding and was eager to sign the guest book. An elderly nun in front of her was taking a long time to sign, and Shelly became impatient. Her father exhorted: "Wait till the nun signs, Shelly."

———◆———

A spoonerism betrays a slip of the tongue, but a far more egregious instance of language abuse is the malapropism, which exposes a slip of the mind. This solecism is named for Mrs. Malaprop, a character in *The Rivals*, a play by Richard Brinsley Sheridan first performed in 1775 at Covent Garden. *Malaprop* comes from the French phrase *mal a propos*, which by 1688 was all jammed together into the English word *malapropos*, meaning "inappropriately." Mrs. Malaprop loves to use big words, and like most people who do so, including your sometimes sesquipedalian author, she sometimes gets them wrong. A true malaprop must be unintentionally used to mean something other than its actual meaning, it must be similar in sound or spelling to the correct word, and it must itself be a real word.

A few of Mrs. M.'s howlers—and they are meant to produce howls of delight from the audience—include:

* "But the point we would request you is, that you will promise to forget this fellow—to illiterate [*obliterate*] him, I say, quite from your memory."
* "I hope you will represent her to the Captain as an object not altogether illegible [*ineligible*]."
* "He is the very pineapple [*pinnacle, epitome?*] of politeness!"
* "She's as headstrong as an allegory [*alligator*] on the banks of the Nile."

Mrs. Malaprop's merriest marathon of muddled misusage occurs in a long speech that has no less than eleven examples:

"I would by no means wish a daughter of mine to be a progeny [*prodigy*] of learning . . . I would never let her meddle with Greek, or Hebrew, or algebra, or simony [*similes?*, *simplisms?*, *harmony?*], or fluxions [*inflections?*, *fractions?*], or paradoxes [*paradigms?*, *parallaxes?*], or such inflammatory [*informative?*, *transitory?*] branches of learning . . . Then, sir, she should have a supercilious [*superb?*, *superior?*, *superficial?*] knowledge in accounts;—and as she grew up I would have her instructed in geometry [*geography*], that she might know something of the contagious [*contiguous*] countries, but above all, Sir Anthony, she should be mistress of orthodoxy [*orthography*], that she might not misspell, and mispronounce words so shamefully as girls usually do; and likewise that she might reprehend [*comprehend*] the true meaning of what she is saying. This, Sir Anthony, is what I would have a woman know;—and I don't think there is a superstitious [*superfluous*] article in it."

—•—

Although Sheridan invented the character from which the word came, malapropisms existed long before Mrs. Malaprop. Shakespeare's characters often indulged in them. Constable Dogberry in *Much Ado About Nothing* assures Leonato, "Our watch, sir, have indeed comprehended two auspicious persons." In the same play, Dogberry observes, "Comparisons are odorous." Launcelot in *The Merchant of Venice* says that Shylock is "the very devil incarnal," and Elbow in *Measure for Measure* refers to criminals as "notorious benefactors" and to a woman of ill repute as one "cardinally given."

One of the modern masters of malapropism is undoubtedly George W. Bush. As president, he made a great many speeches (it goes with the job), in which flagrantly mangled words were often uttered. To be very fair to W., if you insist, some Bushisms represent mere slips of the tongue, rather than attempts to use words that are too big for his breaches. A few choice examples are:

✳ "I'm honored to be here with the eternal general of the United States, mi amigo Alberto Gonzales." (Washington, D.C., May 4, 2007)

✳ "And there is distrust in Washington. I am surprised, frankly, at the amount of distrust that exists in this town. And I'm sorry it's the case, and I'll work hard to try to elevate it." (interview on National Public Radio, January 29, 2007)

✳ "I don't want nations feeling like that they can bully ourselves and our allies. I want to have a ballistic defense system so that we can make the world more peaceful, and at the same time I want to reduce our own nucular capacities to the level commiserate with keeping the peace." (Des Moines, Iowa, October 23, 2000)

✳ "They misunderestimated me." (Bentonville, Arkansas, November 6, 2000)

✳ "They said, 'You know, this issue doesn't seem to resignate with the people.' And I said, you know something? Whether it resignates or not doesn't matter to me, because I stand for doing what's the right thing. . . ." (Portland, Oregon, October 31, 2000)

✳ "A tax cut is really one of the anecdotes to coming out of an economic illness." (*The Edge* with Paula Zahn, September 18, 2000)

✳ "We cannot let terrorists and rogue nations hold this nation hostile or hold our allies hostile." (Des Moines, Iowa, August 21, 2000)

✳ "I thought how proud I am to be standing up beside my dad. Never did it occur to me that he would become the gist for cartoonists." (*Newsweek*, February 28, 2000)

Move over, Mrs. Malaprop!

President Bush is not alone among celebrated individuals in his proclivity for the inappropriate word. A few other examples from the media:

* Cornel West, professor of religion and African American studies, Princeton University: "So, truth has to lie prostate, which means we have to reveal it in its nakedness, even if that nakedness seems to be connected to a lack of power." (September 7, 2007, *Real Time with Bill Maher*)
* Mike Tyson, former heavyweight champion: "I really dig Hannibal. Hannibal had real guts. He rode elephants into Cartilage."
* Jack Dyer, Australian football commentator: "Mark Lee's arms went up like two giant testicles."
* Brandon Rogers, "American Idol" singer: "I made a carnal sin, I forgot my words."

The Web site fun-with-words.com offers an array of malapropisms. Some of their best:

* He had to use a fire distinguisher.
* Dad says the monster is just a pigment of my imagination.
* Isn't that an expensive pendulum around that man's neck?
* Punctuation means not to be late.
* He's a wolf in cheap clothing.
* Michelangelo painted the Sixteenth Chapel.

Similar to the malaprop—and the cause of many of them—is the mondegreen, which is not so much a misuse of words as a mishearing of them. The name was coined by Sylvia Wright in her essay "The

Death of Lady Mondegreen" in *Harper's Magazine* in November, 1954. Wright described how, as a young girl, she misheard the final line from the seventeenth-century ballad "The Bonnie Earl o' Murray." As she recalled, it went:

> Ye Highlands and ye Lowlands,
> Oh, where hae ye been?
> They hae slain the Earl o' Murray,
> And Lady Mondegreen.

What they had done, of course, was to have slain the Earl of Murray and laid him on the green.

A much-quoted example of mondegreens is "Gladly, the cross-eyed bear," supposedly a mishearing of "Gladly the cross I'd bear," from the hymn "Keep Thou My Way, O Lord" by Fanny Crosby. In fact, however, the hymn's original words are "Gladly the cross *I'll* bear." No doubt "I'd" was substituted for "I'll" in some congregations, giving rise to the monde-green. Some people have said there is also a hymn called "The Consecrated Cross I'd Bear," which, of course, is usually heard as "the constipated cross-eyed bear."

Hymns are fertile fields for mondegreens. In Milwaukee, after singing "Jesus Is Seeking A Humble Heart," a child asked his teacher, "Why is Jesus sneaking in Humbolt Park?" (A park of that name does exist in Milwaukee.) The old favorite "Bringing in the Sheaves" is often misunderstood in either one of two ways: "bringing in the sheep," or, more pungently, "bringing in the cheese." And if evidence is needed that the "Battle Hymn of the Republic" helped to preserve and expand this nation, there is the little girl who sang "Glory, glory, Honolulu."

Other favorite mondegreens are:

* "The girl with colitis goes by" ["kaleidoscope eyes"], from the Beatles' "Lucy in the Sky With Diamonds."
* "Double, double, toilet trouble," from *Macbeth.*
* "'Scuse me while I kiss this guy" ["the sky"], from Jimi Hendrix's "Purple Haze."
* "The ants are my friends," from Bob Dylan's "Blowin' in the Wind."
* "Round John Virgin," from "Silent Night."

The recitation of the Pledge of Allegiance to the Flag offers so many opportunities for mondegreens that Jon Carroll at the Web site sfgate.com has created a composite of youngsters' mishearings: "I pledge a lesion to the flag of the United State of America, and to the republic for Richard Stans, one naked individual, with liver tea, and just this for all."

Children are usually the most susceptible mishearers, and one story is told of a minister who found his five-year-old son burying a dead robin. The youngster had put the bird in a small box and dug a hole in which to place it. Before committing the remains to the earth, the boy intoned the prayer, "Glory be unto the Father, and unto the Son, and into the hole he goes."

Closed-captioned live television broadcasting, in which the spoken text is displayed visually on the screen, is a marvelous source of frequent mondegreens. They arise both from the mistakes of human stenotypists who may mishear what is said, as well as from the use of computer software with which an instant choice must be made from a range of possibilities in the computer's stored vocabulary. Or sometimes hurried captioners simply hit the wrong keys. Some mondegreens that have appeared on screen in television news reports include:

* "Classy felonies" [instead of "Class A felonies"]
* "Grandpa raid" ["grand parade"]
* "Firefighters to deal with not just the fire but people in the middle of road ejaculating" ["evacuating"]
* "Less affair" ["laissez faire"]
* "In the hospital with an enlarged prostitute" ["prostate"]
* "For fee hick call axe sedan" ["four-vehicle accident"]

Eggcorns are very similar to mondegreens; in fact, they are really the same thing under another name. They are mishearings of common words or phrases, so-called from someone who thought an acorn was an eggcorn. Some other examples that you're likely to hear are:

* You've got another thing [think] coming.
* Duck [duct] tape
* Mute [moot] point
* Anchors away [aweigh]
* Peak [pique] one's interest

Misheard syllables are similar to what are known as holorimes, meaning a rhyme that encompasses a whole line or phrase. It's really a misnomer, for no actual rhyme is involved. The word describes two juxtaposed lines of homophones or near-homophones that sound alike but have very different meanings—or maybe none at all. If you try very, very hard you can squeeze a wee bit of rationality out of some holorimes, but at least one of the pair in most of the following created by your author sounds like utter drivel.

We're dough-makers and have social opportunities.
Weird dome acres end of sew shell hop or tune at ease.

Grimm airs of grizzly bear atone for sour old bandleader.
Grim heirs of grisly baritone force our rolled banned lieder.

—•◼•—

I always recommend potpourri to some youth in Asia.
Eye awl weighs, wreck, amend popery: twosome
euthanasia.

—•◼•—

We'll see computer pop-up ads no more after this one.
Wheel sea come, pewter paw pup pads Nome or rafter the
swan.

—•◼•—

Law school degrees are too late for teenaged daughters to
benefit.
Loss cooled a grease; our tool ate fourteen aged otters' tube
in a fit.

—•◼•—

Mattel, the ubiquitous toy makers, have even crafted a game
from holorimes. It's called, for want of a better name, Mad Gab, and
the object is for one team to say aloud some words strung together,
ostensibly without any meaning, such as:

1. Ask rude arrive her
2. Bat tree snot ink looted
3. Yore look ink hood
4. Hoe pinup hits depot lease,

and for the other team to guess that the meaning of them is

1. A screwdriver
2. Batteries not included
3. You're looking good
4. Open up! It's the police!

Thug aim miss uh vale Hubble hat tree tale lout
Letts four Hun dearth err tee doll errs, end bat trees ore knot knee
dead.

—•—

Author's question to self: can you imagine anyone
making a living by sitting around thinking up inane
babble like this? Answer: Sure!

—•—

The late actor and word maven Luis d'Antin van Rooten
invented fiendishly clever bilingual holorimes in his delightful
Mots D'Heures: Gousses, Rames (tortuously translated as "Words of
the Hours: Root and Branch," but really meant to be spoken aloud
phonetically and not put into English at all). Van Rooten's game was
to find homophones in French (often archaic) for the English words
of familiar nursery rhymes. For example:

Chacun Gille
Houer ne taupe de hile
Tôt-fait, j'appelle au boiteur.
Chaque fêle dans un broc, est-ce crosne?
Un Gille qu'aime tant berline à fêtard.

Oh, by the way, a rudimentary knowledge of French
pronunciation is required for this to be any fun. An added delight
of Van Rooten's little volume is the pseudo-scholarly annotation that
tries to wrest some meaning from the nonsensical French words.

Trying the same thing in English results in equally nonsensical holorimes, as your author discovered in penning this master-
piece manqué:

Mare he addle lid dull am.
Hits fleas worse wide has know.
Hand if re weareth at mare he wend,
Dell am wash your tug oh.

Hey, Mr. Mattel! Did you catch that nifty restating of "Mary had a little lamb?" No? Well, all right.

In closing, your author would like to leave you with this parting shot of gibberish:

Eye owe pew reel lea in Shaw weed ditch apt her.

CHAPTER EIGHT

GOD SAVE THE QUEENS!

Acrostic Puzzles

Leave writing plays, and choose for thy command
Some peaceful province in Acrostic Land.
There thou may'st wings display and altars raise
And torture one poor word ten thousand ways.

—John Dryden, "Mac Flecknoe"

If racing is the sport of kings, the acrostic may be regarded as the delight of queens. The acrostic puzzle began life as a type of poem in which the initial letters of each line spelled out a word. From the Greek *akrostichis*, meaning "beginning of the line," acrostics have been known since ancient times and, like almost everything else you can think of, enjoyed a renaissance in the sixteenth century. An acrostic was regarded as an ideal form for love poetry, since the name of the beloved could be subtly worked into a poem on any subject, demonstrating simultaneously the writer's admiration for his beloved and his own cleverness. Queen Elizabeth I was honored by many such poems—well, she was the queen, after all—including a series of them by Sir John Davies, although for all his efforts, the thankless queen was not the one who bestowed his knighthood upon him—that came later from King James I, who admired his legal skills even more than his poetry.

Davies's "To the Spring," published in 1599, is a good example of the acrostic verse form:

> Earth is now greene, and heaven is blew,
> Lively Spring which makes all new,
> Iolly Spring, doth enter;
> Sweete yong sun-beames doe subdue
> Angry, agèd Winter;
> Blasts are calme, and seas are milde;
> Every meadow flowes with balme,
> The Earth weares all her riches;
> Harmonious birdes sing such a psalme,
> As eare and heart bewitches.
> Reserve (sweet Spring) this Nymph of ours,
> Eternall garlands of thy flowers,
> Greene garlands never wasting;
> In her shall last our State's faire Spring,
> Now and for ever flourishing,
> As long as Heaven is lasting.

The sharp-eyed reader and perhaps some of you others, too, will notice that the initial letters of each line spell out ELISABETHA REGINA, which is Queen Elizabeth in Latin. Of course, Davies had to resort to spelling "Jolly" with an "I," but as you can tell from the rest of the poem, orthography was not a big deal with the Eliza-

bethans, and the "J" and the "I" in this period were often used interchangeably, as King Iames himself could attest.

The acrostic verse form continued to be a fad for many years, prompting a disgusted John Dryden in the lines quoted above from "Mac Flecknoe" in

1682 to castigate his fellow poet Thomas Shadwell for indulging in what Dryden regarded as a pointless pastime. In the eighteenth century the essayist Joseph Addison also fulminated about the acrostic—as well as the anagram—unable to decide which was the worse abomination. "The acrostic was probably invented about the same time with the anagram," he wrote in *The Spectator* of May 9, 1711, "though it is impossible to decide whether the inventor of the one or the other were the greater blockhead."

Fast-forward to the nineteenth century, when another queen of England, Victoria (heedless of Dryden and Addison's opprobrium), was instrumental in inventing the acrostic puzzle. The following one was devised by the queen herself, maybe with a little input from Prince Albert, and published in 1861:

CLUES:	ANSWERS:
A city in Italy	NapleS
A river in Germany	ElbE
A town in the United States	WashingtoN
A town in North America	CincinnatI
A town in Holland	AmsterdaM
The Turkish name of Constantinople	StambouL
A town in Bothnia	TorneA
A city in Greece	LepantO
A circle on the globe	EcliptiC

The diligently attentive reader (wake up now) will note that this is a two-way acrostic, with the initial letters of the answers reading down spelling the name of an English city (NEWCASTLE) and the final letters reading upward spelling what the city was noted for (COAL MINES).

Way to go, Your Majesty!

Fast-forward again to twentieth-century America, where a former schoolteacher named Elizabeth Kingsley devel-

oped the acrostic form into a new kind of puzzle that she dubbed a "Double-Crostic." It appeared regularly for many years in the pages of the *Saturday Review of Literature*. Mrs. Kingsley, sometimes known fancifully to puzzle aficionados as "Our Queen Elizabeth," constructed a weekly acrostic for the magazine from 1934 until her retirement in 1952. She was succeeded by Doris Wortman and then by Thomas H. Middleton, who continued the puzzles until the magazine's demise in the 1980s. Thereafter Middleton (who was also a Hollywood character actor in such films as *Slappy and the Stinkers*) devised similar acrostic puzzles for the *New York Times*.

The Kingsley Double-Crostic is a puzzle consisting of a grid with numbered blank squares, into which a quotation is to be entered. The letters forming the quotation are to be found in a series of words or phrases to which clues are given. Each letter in the answer words has a number that corresponds to a number listed sequentially in the grid. When the puzzle is complete, not only will you have the completed quotation in the grid but also, the initial letters of the answer words will spell the name of the author of the quotation and the work from which it was taken—or, in the second puzzle that follows here, the birthplace of the author.

Nowadays acrostic puzzles appear in many publications under various names including Quotewords, Crostigrams, and

Wordocrostics, and a free sampling of them can be found at crostix. com. So that you too, dear reader, though probably a mere commoner, and possibly, in Addison's view, a blockhead as well, may enjoy this exquisite queenly pastime, your author thoughtfully provides herewith some acrostic puzzles from his royal treasury. If you've never worked one before, reread the previous paragraph very carefully. Now read it again. Keep in mind that blank squares indicate the ends of words, that words may carry over from one line of the grid to the next, and that punctuation must be inserted in the quote where you think best. On your mark, get set, go!

ACROSTIC PUZZLE

NUMBER ONE

				1 U	2 E	3 B		4 A	5 F	6 B	7 E	8 O			9 D	10 A	11 F		12 V
13 K	14 W	15 A		16 C	17 B	18 K	19 N	20 T	21 I	22 U	23 X	24 X		25 J	26 C		27 B	28 W	29 F
30 D	31 A	32 S	33 C	34 H	35 I		36 G	37 J	38 N	39 T	40 N	41 H	42 Q		43 C	44 D	45 M	46 O	47 B
48 U	49 L	50 Q	51 T	52 R		53 K	54 O		55 J	56 R	57 F		58 D	59 S	60 X	61 C	62 X	63 N	64 D
65 H	66 J		67 L	68 A	69 R		70 W	71 S	72 B	73 P	74 R	75 X		76 W	77 S	78 S		79 T	80 B	81 W
82 X	83 A	84 Q		85 C	86 A	87 X		88 N		89 D	90 O	91 L	92 V		93 D	94 J	95 F	96 R	97 B	98 V
99 C		100 Q	101 R	102 L	103 J		104 V	105 C	106 K	107 L	108 B	109 J	110 F		111 F	112 B		113 O	114 J	115 K
116 A	117 P		118 A	119 U		120 K	121 E	122 C		123 S	124 F	125 J		126 D		127 V	128 G		129 L	130 I
131 N	132 O	133 Q		134 F	135 B		136 Q	137 A	138 M		139 B	140 J	141 W		142 A	143 G	144 T		145 K	146 K
147 D	148 G	149 J	150 P	151 I	152 B	153 N	154 X		155 G	156 D		157 E	158 D	159 N	160 B	161 P	162 J	—	163 X	164 J
165 S	166 C	167 F	168 A	169 N		170 K	171 B	172 F	173 J		174 X	175 A	176 Q		177 H	178 C	179 S	180 J		181 N
182 F	183 O	184 H		185 W		186 C	187 K	188 J	189 A	190 B	191 N	192 P		193 F	194 D		195 J	196 L		197 K
198 X		199 J	200 K	201 C		202 X	203 D	204 V	205 S	206 X	207 I	208 J	209 F		210 P	211 V	212 W	213 M	214 C
215 L		216 B	217 A	218 K	219 M	220 L	221 J		222 Q	223 N	224 F	225 C	226 A						

CLUES

A. __ __ __ __ __ __ __ __ __ __ __ __ __ __ __ __
217 175 68 226 31 4 137 83 118 189 168 116 15 142 86 10

B. __ __ __ __ __ __ __ __ __ __ __ __ __ __ __ __ __
139 97 80 47 160 190 17 112 216 3 171 152 27 135 108 72 6

C. __ __ __ __ __ __ __ __ __ __ __ __ __ __ __
186 61 43 225 85 201 122 33 26 16 105 178 166 99 214

D. __ __ __ __ __ __ __ __ __ __ __ __ __
9 158 58 44 156 30 147 194 126 93 89 203 64

E. __ __ __ __
7 2 157 121

F. __ __ __ __ __ __ __ __ __ __ __ __ __ __ __
124 172 167 209 110 193 182 134 95 57 29 5 224 111 11

A. 1963 British musical satire filmed in 1969 (5 words)

B. Tallulah Bankhead's father's job from 1936-1940 (4 words)

C. Iconic Salinger work (4 words)

D. 1948 Bergman/Laughton/Boyer film (3 words)

E. Cartoonist Goldberg

F. 1941 Lillian Hellman play (4 words)

G. __ __ __ __ __
148 143 128 36 155

H. __ __ __ __ __
34 184 41 177 65

I. __ __ __ __ __
21 130 151 207 35

J. __ __ __ __ __ __ __ __ __ __ __ __ __
37 94 55 103 66 173 114 208 125 149 164 188 180

__ __ __ __ __ __ __
199 195 162 25 109 140 221

K. __ __ __ __ __ __ __ __ __ __ __ __
13 145 170 120 53 106 18 115 197 200 187 218

L. __ __ __ __ __ __ __ __ __
196 67 215 91 220 129 107 49 102

M. __ __ __ __
45 213 219 138

N. __ __ __ __ __ __ __ __ __ __ __ __
40 88 38 131 223 63 181 191 19 159 153 169

O. __ __ __ __ __ __ __
8 54 113 90 132 183 46

P. __ __ __ __ __ __
150 73 117 161 210 192

Q. __ __ __ __ __ __ __ __ __
84 50 222 100 176 42 136 146 133

R. __ __ __ __ __ __
56 74 52 69 101 96

S. __ __ __ __ __ __ __ __ __
59 77 78 165 32 71 179 123 205

T. __ __ __ __ __
144 20 39 79 51

U. __ __ __ __
1 22 48 119

V. __ __ __ __ __ __ __
127 104 211 204 12 98 92

W. __ __ __ __ __ __ __ __
14 185 76 141 70 212 81 28

X. __ __ __ __ __ __ __ __ __ __ __ __ __
87 198 75 202 62 163 82 174 206 154 23 60 24

G. Shakespeare's
feet

H. Lerner's
partner

I. Obsessed,
eccentric

J. Showbiz news show on TV
from 1981 (2 words)

K. Shout of an approving
audience (2 words)

L. Michael
Frayn farce (2 words)

M. Pop of punk

N. First opera of
The Ring (2 words)

O. Attempts, exertions

P. Affirm, authenticate,
swear

Q. Without regard for
legality

R. Rupture

S. Little Bear in the sky
(2 words)

T. Ozawa of the
podium

U. One of Willy Loman's
sons

V. Endeavor

W. Rembrandt Peale vis-à-vis
Rembrandt van Rijn

X. Peter Wimsey's creator
(2 words)

ACROSTIC PUZZLE

NUMBER TWO

						1 O		2 D	3 A	4 M	5 F		6 U	7 K	8 J	9 F	10 S
11 G	12 O		13 T	14 D	15 F	16 Q	17 H	18 L	19 I	20 K	21 R	22 F	23 M	24 H	25 L	26 B	27 S	28 A	29 O
	30 M	31 H	32 G		33 F	34 S	35 J	36 U	37 E	38 B	39 P		40 S	41 H		42 M	43 U	44 G		45 R
46 L	47 J	48 H	49 F	50 K	51 I	52 P	53 R	54 E	55 M	56 F		57 H	58 F	59 E	60 C		61 Q	62 U	63 S	64 J
65 A	66 B	67 M	68 F	69 C	70 V		71 J	72 A	73 V	74 H	75 F	76 M		77 D	78 F	79 U		80 F	81 H
82 A	83 H	84 C	85 L		86 A		87 Q	88 M	89 B	90 U	91 H		92 I	93 F	94 K	95 M		96 K	97 N	98 A
	99 T	100 S	101 M	102 N	103 F		104 B	105 M		106 N	107 G	108 L	109 R	110 M	111 F	112 J	113 R		114 C	115 A
116 G	117 F	118 K		119 H	120 F		121 A	122 D	123 J	124 N	125 M		126 F	127 L	128 M	129 J	130 O		131 I	132 L
133 J	134 R	135 M	136 A		137 Q	138 O	139 M		140 P	141 O	142 F	143 U	144 L	145 M		146 V	147 J	148 B		149 S
150 A	151 E	152 F		153 F	154 J	155 G	156 H		157 H	158 M	159 F	160 Q	161 P	162 V	163 B	164 A	165 D	166 C	167 K	168 T
169 S	170 L	171 L		172 L	173 M	174 T		175 J		176 F	177 H		178 P	179 M	180 B	181 D	182 T	183 G	184 L	185 F
186 H		187 R	188 E	189 L		190 P	191 V	192 S		193 S	194 A	195 J	196 L		197 U	198 K	199 A	200 F	201 L
202 A	203 E		204 H	205 F		206 D	207 H	208 E	209 B	210 A									

CLUES

A. _ _ _ _ _ _ _ _ _ _ _ _ _ _ _ _
3 164 72 202 98 194 121 210 82 150 28 65 199 86 115 136

B. _ _ _ _ _ _ _ _ _
209 89 66 148 163 38 104 180 26

C. _ _ _ _ _
60 166 114 69 84

D. _ _ _ _ _ _ _
14 165 77 206 2 122 181

E. _ _ _ _ _ _ _
37 203 59 188 54 151 208

F. _ _ _ _ _ _ _ _ _ _ _ _ _ _ _ _ _
103 120 205 93 185 22 58 9 153 200 176 49 117 78 68 111 142

_ _ _ _ _ _ _ _ _
80 15 159 126 5 56 33 75 201

A. Dickens novel (5 words)

B. Comic opera by Gilbert & Sullivan

C. Puccini opera

D. Elegant or snobbish (hyphenate)

E. Prima ballerina Galina

F. Musical group founded by Sir Thomas Beecham (3 words)

G. _ _ _ _ _ _ _
107 11 155 183 44 116 32

H. _ _ _ _ _ _ _ _ _ _ _ _ _ _
17 31 91 48 24 119 83 152 41 74 204 186 157 177

_ _ _ _
57 81 156 207

I. _ _ _ _
131 51 92 19

J. _ _ _ _ _ _ _ _ _ _ _ _
133 71 123 175 147 112 64 195 35 154 8 129 47

K. _ _ _ _ _ _ _ _
167 7 50 20 94 198 118 96

L. _ _ _ _ _ _ _ _ _ _ _ _ _ _
196 170 108 132 144 25 184 18 46 189 172 127 85 171

M. _ _ _ _ _ _ _ _ _ _ _ _ _ _
110 101 88 135 23 55 145 95 76 128 179 158 139 105

_ _ _ _ _ _
4 67 125 42 173 30

N. _ _ _ _
102 106 97 124

O. _ _ _ _ _ _
1 130 141 138 29 12

P. _ _ _ _ _ _
161 140 52 178 39

Q. _ _ _ _ _ _
61 16 137 87 160 190

R. _ _ _ _ _ _ _
45 21 187 113 53 109 134

S. _ _ _ _ _ _ _ _ _ _
169 63 10 34 149 192 40 100 27 193

T. _ _ _ _ _
168 174 182 99 13

U. _ _ _ _ _ _ _ _
6 143 43 197 36 62 90 79

V. _ _ _ _ _
162 70 146 73 191

G. Cultured; like fuel oil

H. 1963 Jack Lemmon film
(5 words)

I. J. S., C.P.E., or P.D.Q.

J. Latin phrase that literally
means "There is truth in
wine" (3 words)

K. Dickens or Melville, e.g.

L. With "The," a fairy-tale ballet by Tchaikowsky
(2 words)

M. Play by Shakespeare
(4 words)

N. Nymph who loved Narcissus

O. Moved slowly

P. Slangy "certainly"

Q. American Indian ceremony

R. Student or graduate of
Oxford University

S. Scottish song (2 words)

T. Change for a new use

U. Americas (2 words)

V. First word of title of a play
about Willy Loman

ACROSTIC PUZZLE

NUMBER THREE

					1 C	2 J	3 Q	■	4 B	5 D	6 C	7 A	8 G	■	9 O	10 G
11 R	■	12 B	13 I	14 G	15 H	16 S	17 J	18 W	■	19 E	20 B	21 V	22 J	23 L	24 O	■	25 C	26 U	■	27 C
28 B	29 G	30 P	31 H	32 O	33 S	34 K	35 R	36 J	37 T	■	38 H	39 J	40 B	■	41 H	42 I	43 D	■	44 H	45 C
46 K	47 I	48 F	49 T	50 S	51 L	■	52 K	53 F	■	54 B	55 K	56 D	57 J	58 L	59 I	■	60 O	61 L	62 G	63 U
64 J	65 S	66 I	■	67 U	68 L	69 O	■	70 L	71 R	72 G	73 B	74 D	75 F	76 H	■	77 O	78 B	79 D	80 C	81 P
82 H	■	83 E	84 H	85 W	86 F	87 L	88 D	■	89 F	■	90 M	91 R	92 H	93 B	94 O	■	95 E	96 G	■	97 K
98 U	99 B	■	100 L	101 R	102 B	103 K	■	104 N	105 O	106 M	107 S	108 L	109 S	110 A	111 I	■	112 Q	113 R	■	114 I	115 G
116 O	■	117 Q	118 N	119 G	120 J	■	121 C	122 H	123 G	■	124 J	125 C	126 R	■	127 N	128 H	129 O	130 Q	■	131 U
132 O	133 V	134 W	135 B	136 V	137 J	■	138 L	139 I	140 C	141 H	142 O	143 R	144 S	145 B	146 F	147 D	148 M	■	149 R	150 P
151 T	152 O	153 I	154 B	155 L	156 W	■	157 F	158 I	159 O	160 H	■	161 C	162 F	163 N	■	164 V	165 P	166 M	167 I	168 H
■	169 S	170 K	■	171 B	172 D	173 I	■	174 L	175 I	176 M	■	177 J	178 O	179 I	180 D	■	181 F	182 I	183 H
184 F	185 A	186 V	187 O	188 C	■	189 R	190 W	191 O	192 I	193 S	194 T	■	195 R	196 N	197 L	198 F	199 W	200 H	201 J	202 B
203 G	204 I	■	205 D	206 B	207 O	208 O	209 D	210 T	■	211 A	212 M	213 W	214 Q	■	215 P	216 S	217 R	218 N	219 Q
220 O	■	221 P	222 H	223 C	224 A	225 O	226 L	■	227 V	228 F										

CLUES

A. ___ ___ ___ ___ ___
211 185 224 110 7

B. ___ ___ ___ ___ ___ ___ ___ ___ ___ ___ ___ ___ ___ ___ ___
78 93 202 54 206 102 145 99 20 4 28 135 171 73 40 154 12

C. ___ ___ ___ ___ ___ ___ ___ ___ ___ ___ ___ ___
188 6 80 125 1 140 27 45 121 223 161 25

D. ___ ___ ___ ___ ___ ___ ___ ___ ___ ___ ___ ___
56 205 79 209 88 5 74 172 147 43 180 155

E. ___ ___ ___
19 95 83

F. ___ ___ ___ ___ ___ ___ ___ ___ ___ ___ ___ ___
89 184 198 48 162 86 228 75 146 157 181 53

A. Conductor Zubin

B. Sondheim musical or Mozart serenade (4 words)

C. Soprano who shares a first name with Tebaldi (2 words)

D. The K in K-12

E. London's Old ____

F. Mrs. William Shakespeare (2 words)

God Save the Queens!

G. _ _ _ _ _ _ _ _ _ _
203 72 115 62 10 29 14 123 96 8 119

H. _ _ _ _ _ _ _ _ _ _ _ _ _ _ _ _ _ _
168 200 41 15 183 92 222 122 141 76 160 128 38 44 82 31 84

I. _ _ _ _ _ _ _ _ _ _ _ _ _ _ _ _ _
42 179 192 153 114 111 173 47 59 139 66 158 182 204 175 167 13

J. _ _ _ _ _ _ _ _ _ _ _ _ _ _
36 57 64 2 22 124 17 120 137 177 39 201

K. _ _ _ _ _ _ _
34 97 46 170 52 55 103

L. _ _ _ _ _ _ _ _ _ _ _ _ _ _
226 68 108 70 174 197 58 51 138 100 23 87 61

M. _ _ _ _ _ _
176 212 90 166 148 106

N. _ _ _ _ _ _
118 104 127 196 218 163

O. _ _ _ _ _ _ _ _ _ _ _ _ _ _ _ _
178 220 159 69 116 129 60 77 208 132 105 9 207 142 191

_ _ _ _ _ _
94 24 32 225 152 187

P. _ _ _ _ _ _
30 165 221 150 81 215

Q. _ _ _ _ _ _
3 219 117 214 112 130

R. _ _ _ _ _ _ _ _ _ _ _ _
149 35 217 195 71 126 189 11 113 91 101 143

S. _ _ _ _ _ _ _ _ _ _
33 107 16 109 193 144 65 216 169 50

T. _ _ _ _ _
37 49 151 194 210

U. _ _ _ _ _
98 131 63 26 67

V. _ _ _ _ _ _
21 133 186 227 136 164

W. _ _ _ _ _ _ _
85 213 156 18 134 190 199

G. Musical with "Tea for Two" (3 words)

H. 1966 play by Woody Allen (4 words)

I. Keats poem that begins "My heart aches…"(4 words)

J. Indispensable aide (2 words, one a hyphenate)

K. Ontario site of Loon Dollar Monument (2 words)

L. John Jakes trilogy made into a mini-series (3 words)

M. Became angry (2 words)

N. Telescope in the sky

O. Pulitzer Prize-winning play of 1948 (4 words)

P. "Brush up your Shake-speare, and they'll all ____": Cole Porter

Q. "The Perfect Fool" (2 words)

R. Drury Lane actress (1755-1831) noted for Lady Macbeth (2 words)

S. Greek goddess of the Underworld

T. Side-step

U. Roy of the Grand Ole Opry

V. Theatre critic's report

W. "This scepter'd isle," to John of Gaunt

CHAPTER NINE

TICKLING YOUR RIBALDRY

Double Entendres, Newspaper Headlines, Knock-Knock Jokes

Get thee to a nunnery.

—William Shakespeare, *Hamlet*

Wouldn't you know that the master of the double entendre would turn out to be none other than the master of everything else in the English language—William Shakespeare, the Bawd, er, Bard of Stratford-upon-Avon. A double entendre is a more-or-less French expression for a type of pun—a word or phrase whose primary meaning can be interpreted in a second way, usually salacious. As Eric Partridge in his groundbreaking *Shakespeare's Bawdy* demonstrates with great thoroughness, Shakespeare was exceedingly fond of double entendres, the bawdier the better. Hamlet's taunting imperative to Ophelia cited at the head of the chapter can be understood as urging her to retire from the world, either into a convent amidst pious members of a religious order, or, in the slang of sixteenth-century England, into a brothel amidst ladies of quite a different order.

When Shakespeare really got going, the word play was dazzling and decidedly indecent. Consider this exchange between Hamlet and his school friends Rosencrantz and Guildenstern, who are newly arrived to visit him in Elsinore:

> Hamlet: Good lads, how do you both?
> Rosencrantz: As the indifferent children of the earth.
> Guildenstern: Happy, in that we are not over-happy. On fortune's cap we are not the very button.
> Hamlet: Nor the soles of her shoe?
> Rosencrantz: Neither, my lord.
> Hamlet: Then you live about her waist, or in the middle of her favours?
> Guildenstern: Faith, her privates we.
> Hamlet: In the secret parts of Fortune? O most true, she is a strumpet!

With the words "waist" and "middle," Hamlet personifies Fortune as a woman and directs attention to the most intimate part of her body. Guildenstern then uses the word "privates," ostensibly to say that he and Rosencrantz are ordinary foot soldiers in life, but Hamlet immediately seizes upon it to mean the "secret" or privy parts of Fortune, whom he characterizes as a harlot.

Instances can be found in virtually all the plays, but none quite so blatant as the really down-and-dirty exchange in *Henry V*, which might have been considered too blue even for a twentieth-century burlesque house, as the French Princess Katharine tries to learn English from her lady-in-waiting, Alice. Having learned the names of the body parts elbow, neck, and chin, she asks how to say "foot" and "gown."

> Katharine: *Comment appelez-vous le pied et la robe?*

Alice: *Le foot, Madame; et le count* [gown].

Katharine: *Le foot et le count. O Seigneur Dieu! Ils sont mots de son mauvais, corruptible, gros, et impudique, et non pour les dames d'honneur d'user.*

What the scandalized Katharine says is: "The *foutre* and the *con*. My God! The sounds of these words are bad, corrupt, gross, shameless, and not for honorable ladies to use." Her ear has heard Alice's pronunciation of *foot* and *gown* as the French words *foutre* and *con*, which are crude words, respectively (but not respectably) for sexual intercourse and the female genitalia. The French words are, of course, similar enough to English four-letter equivalents that the groundlings are sure to have had a hearty guffaw at the double entendre.

—◆—

Renaissance songwriters excelled in passing off lyrics that seemed perfectly innocent—but only if you weren't paying very close attention. One good example from the eighteenth century or earlier is "A Lusty Young Smith," supposedly about a hardworking young blacksmith:

> A Lusty young Smith at his Vice stood a Filing,
> Rub, rub, rub, rub, rub, rub in and out, in and out ho;
> When to him a Buxom young Damsel came smiling,
> And ask'd if to Work at her Forge he wou'd go.
>
> Her Husband, she said, could scarce raise up his Hammer,
> His strength and his Tools were worn out long ago;
> If she got her Journey-men, could any blame her,
> "Look here," quoth our Workman, "my Tools are not so."

And once his "iron" is "red-hot enough," he goes to work, to the lady's delight, with a "rub, rub, rub, rub, rub, rub in and out ho!"

—◆—

Another rich source of seemingly innocent lyrics that may be taken two ways is blues music of the 1920s and 1930s. Andy Razaf's lyrics in one popular ditty feature a woman chastely observing, supposedly about a chair:

> If I can't sell it, I'm gonna sit down on it.
> I ain't gonna give it away.
> Now darling if you want it, you're gonna have to buy it.
> And I mean just what I say.
> Now how would you like to find this waitin' at home for you every night,
> Only been used once or twice but it's still nice and tight!

It really doesn't take an excessively dirty mind to realize the song might be about something besides a piece of secondhand furniture.

The most delightfully enjoyable double entendres are those made unintentionally. As most men's minds hover near the gutter much of the time, the prevalence of utterances taken to mean something other than intended is not surprising. Charles Dickens himself fell victim to such a lapse when he wrote in *Martin Chuzzlewit*: "She touched his organ, and from that bright epoch, even it, the old companion of his happiest hours, incapable as he had thought of elevation, began a new and deified existence."

He is referring to the reaction of Tom Pinch when he hears a young lady singing, and no doubt the "organ" referred to, elevated or not, was closer to what the *Oxford English Dictionary* calls "a mental or spiritual faculty regarded as an instrument of the mind or soul." Yeah, tell that to the boys in the back room.

Those old nemeses—live radio and television—have produced some classic double entendres. A BBC announcer covering the Oxford-Cambridge boat race rhapsodized: "Ah, isn't that nice. The wife of the Cambridge coach is kissing the cox of the Oxford crew."

A female TV news anchor, commenting to the weatherman on his previous evening's forecast of a snowstorm that failed to materialize, opened the newscast by asking him: "So, Bob, where was that eight inches you promised me last night?"

The picture on the screen was probably a bit wobbly for a few seconds as the camera operators convulsed in laughter.

A favorite pastime of certain British wags, many of whom your author must admit are among his acquaintances, is a verbal game called "As the Actress Said to the Bishop." Relatively harmless persiflage, it requires a quick response to an innocuous remark that with only a little ingenuity can be heard as something dripping with sexual innuendo. Someone might say while moving a piece of furniture, for example, "It's too big to fit," to which the fastest joker within earshot quickly responds, "As the actress said to the bishop." Or referring to an easy task: "It's not hard" (as the actress said to the bishop, heh heh). Playing this game, of course, presupposes a degree of loose morals that is unlikely to be endemic among all actresses and all bishops; but one never knows, do one?

Newspaper headlines can offer unintentional double entendres. Pity the beleaguered copy editor who has to write the headlines in a daily newspaper at lightning speed and under extremely tight space constraints. The goal of the headline is to relate the gist of the story over which it appears and at the same time intrigue the reader to keep reading. Under these conditions, it is no wonder that a few ludicrous double entendres slip by in the frenzy to meet a deadline—although it strains credulity to think that the editors who approved this one weren't aware of what they were doing:

Textron Makes Offer
To Screw Company's
Board and Stockholders

Other inadvertent (well, one supposes they are) newspaper headlines have proclaimed such double entendres as:

Chef Puts His Heart
In Meals for the Needy

How to Lick Pesky
Sores on Your Dog

Valuable Pieces
Of Rock Hudson
Sold at Auction

Dean of Men Will Stop
Drinking on Campus

Half of All Children
Score Below Average

Old Boston Secretary Gives
Furniture Experts a Thrill

And one of the author's favorites, about a pious pilgrim who had a moving religious experience at the Vatican:

Nun Tells How Pope
Touched Her During
Her Visit to Rome

It may not qualify as a headline per se, or even as a double entendre, but there is a map circulated by a chamber of commerce in the Destin, Florida, area that has one of the most exquisite typographical errors ever committed. It shows the location of the "Hospital of the Scared Heart."

Accidental double entendres are something to be avoided, but purposeful punning in newspaper headlines is one of the means that hardworking copy editors use to let off a little steam and tweak their bosses' stuffy blue noses. Some publishers in the front office take a dim view of this playfulness, and the *San Antonio Express-News* went so far as to ban any kind of pun in a headline after a series of them in one week culminated with:

Mumps Outbreak Swells

Part of your author's misspent career was on the copy desk of a now-defunct daily newspaper, whose editor actually delighted in headline puns, under the probably mistaken impression that they encouraged people to read further. An account of a wedding disrupted by the best man's slight wounding of the groom in a gun brawl drew a series of headlines for successive editions throughout the day. The choicest of these were:

Best Man Takes
A Parting Shot

Here Comes the Bride—
Lay That Pistol Down!

———•———

One that didn't make it into the paper, owing to the inexplicable prudery of the news editor, was:

Shotgun Wedding?
Best Man Takes
Aim at the Groom

———•———

Another effort that failed to pass the news editor's scrutiny involved a report that the Lutheran Church had completed a membership census, which had been delayed for several months by administrative problems. The unused headline:

Lutherans Finally
Come to Their Census

———•———

The late copy editor Charles E. Murray, who deftly plied his trade for both the *Houston Press* and the *Houston Chronicle*, won an award for his headline over a story about the dilemma of Arkansas Governor Orval Faubus in his attempt to delay integration of Little Rock's Central High School:

Faubus Between
Little Rock and
A Hard Place

Murray was also reputedly the author of another very politically incorrect zinger that never saw print, concerning an inmate at the state institution for the criminally insane who raped a female employee and escaped. The impish headline no one ever read was:

Nut Screws
And Bolts

Murray's colleague, the late Jim Norton, came up with a lively head for a story about a South American condor, an enormous carrion bird with a wingspan of ten feet, which had escaped from the zoo. The cautionary headline:

Giant Condor Loose—
Better Look Alive!

The *New York Daily News* is noted for two plays on the same words that found their way into headlines. One was on a story about the heiress Gloria Vanderbilt, who was ill in California but intended to fly to New York anyway in order to testify in a lawsuit. The *News's* elegant headline:

Sick Gloria
In Transit
Monday

Some while later, perhaps it was the same copy editor who was assigned to write a headline for a story that reported the end of a Manhattan subway strike just in time for the start of the work week. The result:

Sick Transit's
Glorious Monday

Gold, silver, and bronze medals go to three winners. In third place, a newspaper account of tennis champion Björn Borg's umpteenth victory drew this heading:

Bjorn Again!

—•—

Time Magazine headed a story about the Russian dog named Laika who was sent up into space as a passenger on the Soviet Union's *Sputnik II*:

Mighty Laika Rose

—•—

And the grand prize goes to a headline on a review of a New York musical show that was to have starred the actress Gloria DeHaven, but on opening night featured instead an understudy who was not up to par:

Ain't Miss DeHaven

—•—

Every child knows a few knock-knock jokes, which have produced some of the most outrageous puns ever heard. You probably have not heard the following, however, since they were devised by your author only yesterday.

—•—

Knock-knock. Who's there? Dmitri. Dmitri who?
Dmitri quires cooking at 375 degrees.

—•—

Oooh! But there's more! Here's who's there:

Irene: Irene egotiated the terms of the contract.
Burton: Burton the hand is worth two in the bush.
Sherwood: Sher wood like to have a date with you.
Anderson: . . . Anderson and der Holy Ghost, Amen.
Ernestine: Ernestines do better in school than lazy ones.
Stu Wendell: Stu Wendell little hand points to twelve and
the big hand points to two.

Bertha: Bertha Funation.
Tammany: Tammany cooks spoil the broth.
Denise: Denise are the first things to go.
Natasha: Natasha Stranger.
Alma: Alma Exes Live in Texas.
Marian: Marian haste, repent at leisure.
Andy: Andy walks with me, Andy talks with me, Andy tells
me I am his own.
Emily: Emilyvin' on a jet plane.

Author's note to self: *Knock-knock. Who's there? Aloysius. Aloysius who? Aloysius you'd finish this flummery
and move on to something else.* Consider it done.

CHAPTER TEN

NONSENSE FOR THE NONCE

Verse for Special Occasions

Monday Uncle Fred is eighty-nine,
Would you kindly come up with a line
Or two to help him celebrate?
Something warm and funny's what we need,
I know you turn them out with lightning speed;
We'll start at seven—don't be late.

—Your author

One of the great Hollywood lyricists—it may have been Sammy Cahn—who grew weary of being asked to come up with clever nonce verses for friends' birthdays, anniversaries, retirements, and what-have-you, once threatened (jocosely, it is presumed) to begin charging for these writing services. When asked how much his fee would be, say, for a short birthday poem, he estimated that $25,000 ought to be about right. That's understandable when you realize that figure represents only a fraction of what he might have earned for the same effort in turning out lyrics for such Oscar-winning hits as "Three Coins in the Fountain," "High Hopes," "All the Way," and "Call Me Irresponsible." Few other professions are faced with frequent requests to donate their services to extol an honoree for the entertainment of his or her guests.

Singers and instrumentalists, it's true, may sometimes be asked to render a favorite number or two. However, accountants are not usually asked to balance a bank book, and gastroenterologists are rarely importuned to perform a colonoscopy on the birthday boy or girl (although the latter would likely be far more entertaining than several stanzas of the usual ragged doggerel). Still, your author is regularly pursued, as poetically revealed.

—•—

Oh, and while you're at it, could you write
A little poem and read it Friday night
At Cousin Nell's retirement party?
She'd be so pleased by something nice and gentle,
Warm, sincere, and fairly sentimental,
Short and sweet—and not too arty.
You must think I have a lot of cheek,
To ask for something else—you know, next week
We'll need just one more little rhyme,
Because our LeRoy's going to graduate.
Do something clever he'll appreciate.
And thanks a lot—until next time!

—•—

The word *nonce* comes from the Middle English phrase *for the nones*, meaning "for one, particular, present purpose"; in other words, something created just for the time being. Like fresh caviar, nonce verse is highly perishable and very few examples can survive the occasion for which they were created. It is extremely difficult for them to have a life outside the narrow context that gave them meaning, since they are typically replete with inside jokes and allusions to names and happenings recognizable only to a small coterie.

For maximum effect, nonce verse should be recited aloud, preferably by the author, to a small group, ideally with several strong drinks inside them. Without extensive rehearsal, only the poem's author can successfully convey the necessary emphasis to make the epigrammatic lines zing—and also negotiate the sometimes rather peculiar rhymes and meters that may crop up in order to add to the fun.

With those caveats, a few examples of your author's evanescent works follow. First a few Scandinavia-inspired lines for a celebrant who happened to find herself on a cruise in a Norwegian fjord on her birthday.

MY KINGDOM FOR A NORSE

When your birthday rolls around,
And you're in a foreign region,
The best spot that you could have found
Is someplace that's Norwegian.

Perhaps last week your mood was bad,
Oh, yes, I hear it *was* low.
But now you're cheerful, happy, glad,
And somewhere north of Oslo.

So let us have some birthday fun,
Be sure we tuck our bibs in,
Here in the land of Midnight Sun,
And Grieg, and Munch, and Ibsen.

Norway views its folk with pride,
Although there are not many:
Knute Rockne, Eric Sevareid,
Liv Ullman, Sonia Henie.

Now celebrate with sirloin steak,
Fresh from the grill and sizzling,
And then a piece of birthday cake—
Oops, I didn't mention Quisling.

Forget about him—give a cheer,
Just yell right out the doorway,
Spread the news both far and near,
It's your birthday here in Norway!

Outdoor theaters are great summertime fun—for audiences,
performers, and some of the creepy-crawlers that such gatherings
under the stars always attract. Here are some lines penned on the
occasion of the opening of the summer season at such a starlit play-
house.

THE THEATRE BUGS

To Miller Outdoor Theatre
The show-biz insects swarm
For summer is a-comin' in
And nights are getting warm.

They're veteran performers who
Have trod the boards for years,
And now they haunt the theater
To hear applause and cheers.

Look 'round you as you sit there and
Celebrities you'll see—
A coloratura Cockroach and
A ballerina Bee.

A Mosquito who played Hamlet and
A Moth who danced Giselle
Trade tales with Jiminy Cricket—O,
The stories they can tell!

A pious Praying Mantis who
Once had a stellar role—
A Mantis for All Seasons—
Now chats with Gnat King Cole.

You might see Madame Butterfly,
The star of *Charley's Ant*,
Perhaps a graying Silverfish
Who outshone Cary Grant.

A troupe of thespic Termites show
Just how they chew the scenery,
And there's a Grasshopper who hums
His way through "Mountain Greenery."

A Bolshoi Ballet Centipede
Famed for her arabesque.
Flirts with a Fruitfly who was Top
Banana in burlesque.

A Flea straight from the circus hails
A Mite who starred in *Rent*.
That Scorpion's their agent, and
He'd kill for ten percent.

Perhaps four famous Beetles might
Stop by to sip some tea
And play their song that first went gold,
"Larva, Come Back to Me."

A Wasp who used to buzz around
With Barrymores and Lunts
Admires a Spider who can play
An octave all at once.

A Yellow jacket tenor sings
A chorus of "Blue Moon,"
Joined by a flighty Firefly
Whom Friml taught to croon.

A dancing Caterpillar greets
A Thrips who plays punk rock,
A Dragonfly who whistles, and
A Wood tick from Woodstock.

A Hollywood-type Hornet's here—
He wowed 'em in *The Sting*.
And look!—a Locust tenor who
Sang Siegfried in *The Ring*.

So at the outdoor theater
When critters start to crawl,
Think twice before you swat one and
Please pause as you recall

These bugs are show-biz legends who
Have come from near and far—
And if you swat an insect, why
You might destroy a star!

—•—

Machu Picchu is a wondrous place high in the Peruvian Andes, a sacred city built by the Incas long before Columbus reached the shores of the New World. Visiting the site can be a mystical experience, and it has inspired many glowing accounts, not the best of which is this meandering whimsicality.

In Machu Picchu
I'll meet and greet you,
And when I've got you
Where I can watch you,
Then I'll beseech you
To let me teach you
In Machu Picchu.

Ay, caramba!
The Urubamba
Is where I think a
Dancing Inca
Will do the samba
And then the mambo
In Ollantaytambo.

Don't be wuss, go
By way of Cuzco,
We'll down a pisco
In some dim disco,
Then have some couscous
Among the standees
High in the Andes.

And as the booze flows
You'll find your fuse blows.
Till some Peruvian
Who's antediluvian
Takes you to Lima
Upon a llama
To end this drama.

—◆—

Wedding anniversaries, especially the twenty-fifth, fiftieth, seventy-fifth, and, no doubt, the one-hundredth, certainly call for memorialization in verse. Whether they call for this kind of theme with variations is another matter:

Aphrodite and Adonis
Were renowned among the Greeks
As quintessential lovers with
Divinely statuesque physiques.
But Fate had no regard at all
For lovey-dovey luminaries,
And sent Adonis down to Hades,
While Aphrodite nuzzled Ares.

Romeo and Juliet
Were dazzling darlings of the stage.
They felt their burning, yearning passion
Would endure more than an age.
But fie upon't! These youthful lovers
Did not for long remain alive,
When Shakespeare found that he required
A tragic ending for Act Five.

Abelard and Eloise
Knew no constraints to their desire,
Their oh-so-passionate lovemaking
Gave off sparks as hot as fire.
But Eloise went to a convent,
Where they cut off all her hair.
And what they cut off Abelard. . . .
Perhaps we'd better not go there.

The two of you are famous, too,
A noted couple of renown.
And when it comes to lasting love,
Why, you can surely claim the crown!
Unlike those other flighty pairs,
Who all had rather brief careers—
The two of you can celebrate
Your fifty very nifty years!

—◆—

When all else fails, steal a song. The following lyric, for a writer celebrating publication of her first novel, is to be sung, if desired, to a melody appropriated from the works of Cole Porter. You'll know which one from the first line.

You're the top!
You're the Queen of Fiction
You're the top,
Without contradiction.
We just know you'll go
On to win a Nobel Prize!
And from here to Boston,
You're our Jane Austen
We lionize!
You're the top,
With a new best-seller,
You're the top—
And a darn good speller,
As for Hemingway,
He's a bit passé,
A flop,
Mr. Hemingway, make way,
'Cause you're the top!

You're the top—
But those big advances
Never stop
If you write romances.
If you tried, then you'd
Beat the best of Judith Krantz,
And Danielle Steel,
After you, we feel
Wouldn't stand a chance!
You're the top,
And you must remember,

Every shop
By about November
Will be tired of art,
They'll want Barbara Cart-
-land slop—
Better crank out some romances,
Stay on top!

And when you're on to a good thing, stick with it. Same song, second time around, this one for the ninetieth birthday of an opera singer (who graciously listened uncomplainingly as it was sung to her by a non–opera singer).

You're the top,
You're a Verdi aria,
You're the top,
And you couldn't be starrier,
You're the stirring sound
That is found in Wagner's *Ring*,
You're the great Puccini,
And the late Rossini—
You're Rudolf Bing!
You're high C
From a fine soprano,
You're a key
On Rubinstein's piano,
I'm a lowly super,
You're a trouper
Who won't stop—

And if, dearie, I'm the bottom,
You're the top!

You're the top,
You're a Roger Federer,
You're the top,
And you're getting betterer,
You're the wit and flash
That's in Ogden Nash's rhymes.
You're a Shakespeare drama,
You're Barack Obama,
You're the *New York Times*!
You're a book
Bound in fine morocco,
You can cook
A divine corn taco,
Like an old bassoon
That's out of tune,
I'll stop.
But if, dearie, I'm the bottom,
You're the top!

—◆—

One mustn't omit the last nonce verse of all, otherwise known as an epitaph. This one—of, by, and for the author—is intended for use in a much-distant future:

The author (Jim Bernhard) departed this life
With the hope there would be an encore.
He's survived by two daughters, a son, and a wife,
And of friends perhaps three or four score.

As these kith and these kinfolk converge 'round the pall,
In the crowd for his last big event,
It's his hope that no one who is there has the gall
To inquire which direction he went.

But he knows very well, as they gather en masse,
To observe the blunt fact he has passed,
It will be hard to tell who is sighing "Alas,"
And who (sotto voce) "At last!"

CHAPTER ELEVEN

INTO THE CRYPT I CREEP

Cryptic Puzzles

You need not mean what you say, but you must say what you mean.
—Alistair Ferguson Ritchie (Afrit of *The Listener*)

While the mentally edentulous still have their pabulum,
the cerebrally dentiferous can now demand a choice of daily bread
into which they can really get their teeth.
—Edward Powys Mathers (Torquemada of the *Observer*)

You have to be a lunatic with a distorted mind to do it.
—Derrick Somerset Macnutt (Ximenes of the *Observer*)

The subject of the above observations is the cryptic cross-word puzzle, sometimes referred to as "British-style." The observers (two of whom in fact worked for the British newspaper the *Observer*) were constructors, or "setters" as the English call them, of the fiendishly difficult puzzles that baffle many Americans and delight their British cousins. The reason for the bafflement and the delight is the same: that the clues to the answers in cryptic puzzles are not straightforward definitions, as literal-minded Americans are accustomed to, but purposely misleading puns, anagrams, and other tricky verbal devices, which the clever Brits lap up like treacle pudding.

Despite the interest of British queens in acrostics from the sixteenth century onward, the British didn't get interested in crossword puzzles until about a decade after they became popular in the United States. The Brits—noted for such peculiarities as pronouncing "Cholmondely" as if it were spelled "Chumley," driving on the left side of the road, and unapologetically mixing lemon squash with their beer—found American clues too mundane and wanted something more quizzical.

Edward Powys Mathers, a critic and translator of Asian poetry, used his scholarly learning to devise mentally punishing clues for puzzles, of which he published several in a weekly journal. His work appeared under the pen name Torquemada, the Spanish Grand Inquisitor, which gives you some idea of how much torture the puzzles were thought to inflict upon the solvers. In 1926 the *Observer*, one of England's leading daily newspapers, commissioned him to do regular puzzles, which he continued until his death in 1939.

By 1930, Queen Mary herself having given crosswords the imprimatur of her royal approval, the stately *Times* decided that it, too, needed a puzzle and found a young farmer and novelist named Adrian Bell to set them along the same lines as Torquemada. The direct successor of Torquemada was Derrick Somerset Macnutt, a classics master, who took over the puzzles at the *Observer* in 1939

under the name Ximenes (also a figure in the Spanish Inquisition) and continued until his death in 1972. Today virtually every British newspaper has a puzzle of this type. Even a few American publications—notably the *New York Times*, the *New York Post*, the *New Yorker*, *Harper's*, *Atlantic Monthly*, and *New*

York, all of them, you notice, in the effete, elite East—have featured them at one time or another.

Two adept American practitioners of the cryptic art are the Broadway lyricists Stephen Sondheim and Richard Maltby, Jr., who would readily agree, if asked, that the discipline of puzzle construction is not unlike that of fitting words to the music of songs. Books of excruciatingly difficult puzzles by both Sondheim and Maltby are available wherever products for mental masochists are sold.

Before you get started on the cryptics provided by your author, a primer may be in order for those of you not familiar with how the clues work. There are some rules. Almost always, the actual straightforward definition of the answer is stated somewhere in the clue, although it is usually accompanied by a secondary hint meant to confuse. The secondary hint may be a pun, an anagram, a homonym, or some even more outrageous verbal device. Some typical examples:

ANAGRAMS

Clue: "Real crazy king."

Answer: LEAR.

"Real" is an anagram of "Lear." Note that when the clue is an anagram of a word or phrase whose letters are to be rearranged, there is usually some indication of that fact, in this case the word "crazy." Other words signaling an anagram might be "clumsy," "odd," "confused," "broken," "disturbed," "wild," "mixed," "demolished," and so on.

CHARADES

Clue: "Canonized trooper is an unknown person."

Answer: STRANGER.

In the charade clue, the word is broken up into its component parts and each part is defined separately. In this case the "trooper" is a "ranger," and he is "canonized" as indicated by the letters "St." (for "saint"), yielding the definition of "an unknown person." A more complicated charade clue might be: "Musical instruments put mother on edge by degrees." Answer: MARIMBAS. *Ma*=mother, *rim*=edge, *BAs*=degrees.

<hr>

TWO MEANINGS

Clue: "Complain about seafood."

Answer: CRAB.

The word "crab" has two meanings. Another clue that has two words with double meanings: "Filming leading actor is meteoric phenomenon." Answer: SHOOTING STAR.

<hr>

REVERSALS

Clue: "Snap back for bad reviews."

Answer: PANS.

"Pans," a theater term for unfavorable criticisms, is "snap" spelled backward. Indications of reversal are usually provided by such words as "back," "backward," "in reverse," "wrong way," or, in the case of vertical answers, "up," "upward," "ascending," or "rising." Another example of a reversal: "Dennis, undergoing setback, strayed." Answer: SINNED. If the answer were in a vertical position in the grid, the clue might read: "On arising, Dennis strayed."

<hr>

BEHEADINGS OR NO ENDINGS

Clue: "Headless maid is a help."

Answer: AID.

"Maid," beheaded, that is losing its initial letter, becomes "aid" ("help"). An example of the loss of an ending might be the clue: "Take a deep breath of yearning, there's no end in sight." Answer: SIGH. Sometimes the missing letter or letters may come in the middle of the word, instead of the beginning or ending. Clue: "I leave obvious map." Answer: PLAIN. Remove "I" from "plain" ("obvious") and the remaining letters are "plan," meaning "map."

INSERTING OR ADDING LETTERS

Clue: "I'm in California briefly for spy agency."
Answer: CIA.

Instead of removing letters, the clue may invite you to add them. "California briefly" is the abbreviation "CA," into which "I" is inserted to yield the answer. Clue: "Do put me on top of building." Answer: DOME.

HOMOPHONES

Clue: "Animal can easily tire, I hear."

Answer: BOAR.

"Boar" is a homophone of "bore." Phrases like "I hear," "it is said," "reportedly," or "sounds like" are usually indications of a homophone.

HIDDEN LETTERS

Clue: "Singer found in rotten orchard."
Answer: TENOR.

The letters of "tenor" are found in "rot*ten or*chard." Usually the words "in," "inside," "within," "contain," "embrace," "swallow," "surround," or some other indication will precede or immediately follow the words in which the hidden letters are to be found.

CONTAINERS

Clue: "Conveying Sir Rudolf's acceptance of Wagnerian cycle."

Answer: BRINGING.

Sir Rudolf refers to opera impresario Rudolf Bing, and the Wagnerian cycle is the "Ring," the letters of which are contained as follows: *B-ring-ing.* Just as with hidden letters, containers usually offer a clue that some letters are to be found within others; in this case it is the word "acceptance" that provides the hint. Other indicators might be "include," "embrace," "inside," or "swallow."

INITIALS.

The answer may be spelled out by the initial (or sometimes final) letters of words in the clue.

Clue: "At first some types of rain may rage."

Answer: STORM.

Indicated by the hint "at first," the initial letters of "some types of rain may" spell the word STORM, which means "rage." To use final letters, the clue might be "Finally, folks want to hear him rage," producing STORM from the last letters of "folks want to hear him."

ABBREVIATIONS, SIGNS, AND SYMBOLS

Some words may be used in the clue that appear in the answer as

symbols or abbreviations. For example the word "love" in a clue may (or may not) refer to the tennis score of zero, which would indicate an "O" in the answer. Common abbreviations are often used: "right" and "left" may mean an "R" and an "L" in the answer. "Points," as in points on the compass could refer to the letters N, S, E, or W. The word "note" in a clue might refer to the letters in the musical scale. "Soft" might indicate a "P" (the musical notation) and "loud" an "F." Numbers may refer to the letters in their Roman equivalents; "ten" might be "X" and "five" "V" in the answer. Every element of the clue must be carefully examined for this kind of symbolism. The answer ALB, for example, might be clued as "priest's vestment is a pound or less." An alb is vestment, and the letters "LB" are an abbreviation of "pound"; the phrase "or less" indicates that it is an abbreviation.

PUNCTUATION

Most internal punctuation marks such as periods and commas can be disregarded, since they are often used to misdirect you—but an exclamation point at the end of a clue may indicate something exceptionally tricky in that clue requiring adroit mental detective work. Similarly, a question mark may suggest that the meaning of the clue as a whole should be considered, usually as an extended pun, without analyzing its individual components.

More than one of these devices may be used in a single clue. Answers may be more than one word, and the number of letters in each word of the answer is given in parentheses following the clue. Punctuation and capitalization may be, and probably are, intended to mislead. Unlike American-style puzzles, there are unkeyed squares, that is, letters in some words do not cross with other words.

Now, sink your teeth into these—and remember as Ximenes said, you have to be a lunatic with a distorted mind to do it.

CRYPTIC

CROSSWORD PUZZLE NUMBER ONE

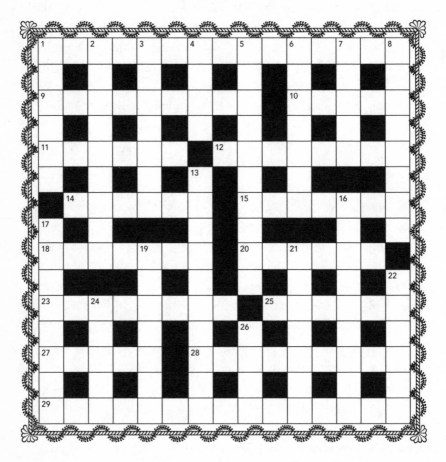

ACROSS

1 Tourist attraction's state-built foyer destroyed (6,2,7)

9 Vegetable paintings I smother (9)

10 Roiled? O, no! But stirred up just the same (5)

11 Addled pro in set back turns to figures of speech (6)

12 Author redistributes the lands (8)

14 Iranian, injured and missing an eye, discovers mythical land (6)

15 Before row, King Cole is more smartly dressed (7)

18 Love between old Egyptian king and Communist is privately taught (7)

20 Damon's upset by wanderers (6)

23 Lying heroic poem in Wagnerian cycle (8)

25 Cupid's beloved has personality (6)

27 By the sound of it, evaluate Bonnie or John (5)

28 Lasting longer than broken violin gut (9)

29 Rule for a park or a narc? (4,3,3,5)

DOWN

1 Athens's foe seems particularly astute ruling the area at first (6)

2 Ride or rider in space (9)

3 Uncle Andy for the most part is nasty (7)

4 Something in the air—good or bad (4)

5 Officer in place above occupant (10)

6 Saloon has wrong tone for minor nobleman (7)

7 Emerson seen in immoral photograph—where's Waldo? (5)

8 Yes, older, confused Alpine singers (8)

13 Solo Australian dog very loudly making football play (7,3)

16 Asian territory resettled in old chain, left out (9)

17 Begin about a thousand TV series (4,4)

19 Riots to disrupt course in Italy (7)

21 Absent, so miss gin cocktail (7)

22 Trims shrubbery (6)

24 First choice (5)

26 If it chafes inside, scratch it (4)

CRYPTIC

CROSSWORD PUZZLE NUMBER TWO

ACROSS

7 China porn keeps Alice upset (9)

8 Billy—with rouge on, that would be capital! (5)

10 Eight pints for Miss Chaney (6)

11 Noble Italian cases not repacked (8)

12 Salve makes messy tint on me (8)

14 Misrepresents flag (6)

15 Fancy basic sonar stirred up California estuary (3,9,3)

18 Suit brought by Rubik in Ireland (6)

19 Violent, ripped off acid (8)

22 Footwear indicates contempt about Alaska, briefly (8)

24 Chaperone due to Ann coming back (6)

25 Valuable possession like television (5)

26 Actor has cat or turkey on voyage (3,6)

DOWN

1 Militia start on a disorganized oppressive rule (15)

2 CEO, confused by vacant land, spotted cat (6)

3 A thousand spear gander (6)

4 Record set in Hindi scribbling (4)

5 John of England's underwater disaster (8)

6 Contrition saves imperfect nature lover (15)

9 Raps at the fort, I hear (6)

13 Surrounded by diplomacy I understood (5)

16 Greek goddesses assemble inside warships (8)

17 Up in Mata Hari's enclave (6)

20 Edit Communist measure (6)

21 A place in the street (6)

23 Destroyed posh boutique (4)

CRYPTIC

CROSSWORD PUZZLE NUMBER THREE

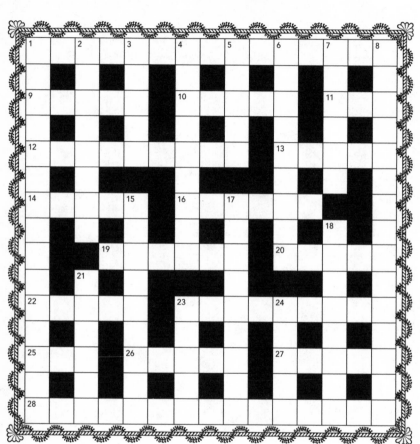

ACROSS

1 U.S. standard Communist, colorless and sad (3,5,3,4)
9 Little colonel on the mark (5)
10 Economize in mask impersonator wore (5)
11 Imitate pea soup (3)
12 Consequence of following arithmetic! (9)
13 Viewed, one hears, as part of the play (5)
14 Dread? In a way, but challenge accepted (5)
16 Moved slowly, chin broken by little editor (6)
19 Separation makes one ill playwright (6)
20 Smoothes beaches (5)
22 At first turquoise, opal, pearl, amethyst, zircon— and then another gem (5)
23 Log on, ride in a storm with this boatman (9)
25 Getting doc off drink would get publicity (3)
26 The Cockney's thanks in letter from Greece (5)
27 No tag changed for dance (5)
28 Mean scene hinted awkwardly for comic kid (6,3,6)

DOWN

1 Her chart hid dirt scattered for titled Shakespearean villain (7,3,5)
2 Procrastinating destroyed dairy lot (8)
3 Prize found in Idaho, North and South Dakota (5)
4 Conductor in Tosca in chaos (9)
5 Islam is holding religious group (5)
6 Forecasters see pest amid doers (9)
7 E-sales reconstitute rents (6)
8 Once geezer's robe is rumpled, he becomes a miser (8, 7)
15 It zoned it wrong for Italian composer (9)
17 London ace destroys columns (9)
18 Emblem is in sign I asked for (8)
21 Broken pens O.K. for this kind of communication (6)
23 Hear, hear! Supposed visitor (5)
24 Bizarre route. That is bizarre! (5)

CRYPTIC

CROSSWORD PUZZLE NUMBER FOUR

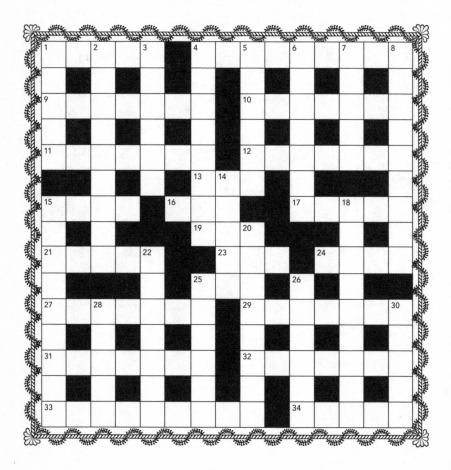

ACROSS

1 English composer spills lager (5)

4 Sex pad due renovation for pair in ballet (3,2,4)

9 Strings of islands? (7)

10 A trip Al ruined, uncompleted (7)

11 Madame, rats are back around you! Speak hesitantly (7)

12 Hip Goth refashions kind of sneaker (4–3)

13 Take it or leave it, Japanese city is in (3)

15 Massage each pain (4)

16 Outlaw saloon (3)

17 Disney film in memorandum boring (5)

19 Lolita gives it a rest— that's funny! (3)

21 Tangled Ascot opera (5)

23 Pipe man up from nap (3)

24 Look! Lego is broken (4)

25 Specified circle (3)

27 Go to bar? Me first backing prohibition (7)

29 Whipped cream, perhaps, is excellent (7)

31 Oh no! Red wacko is venerated (7)

32 Crazy Oscar is around, I see, reportedly in French island (7)

33 Reeds that might blow in forest breezes (9)

34 Stirred what a wok easily holds (5)

DOWN

1 Queues aimlessly without direction in horse play (5)

2 Jumbles you hear in galoshes jumbled (8)

3 Hem, sir, is ragged in French cathedral city (6)

4 Pert liar is confused before the case is heard (8)

5 Poet caught in winesap phobia (6)

6 Angered, changed, but still angered (7)

7 Exit south, in short, to be real (5)

8 Instrument dissects phoney lox (9)

14 Metaphor in Metro personnel (5)

15 I wear hats improperly for big band leader (5,4)

18 Venetian nobleman in magic of pandemonium (9)

20 The French cover attic with trellises (8)

22 Hair crew-cut off the top for plane personnel (7)

25 Soaked so sudden? Not us! (6)

26 Resort contains art of ancient Greek city (6)

28 For this job an out-of-tune musical instrument is obtained (5)

30 Thanks, Princess (5)

CRYPTIC

CROSSWORD PUZZLE NUMBER FIVE

ACROSS

1 CIO brick to crumble for literary reviewer (4,6)

6 God, Dino, straighten out! (4)

10 Heavens! Ecologically correct grazing lands? (5,8)

11 Watchword in human tragedy (6)

12 Resents crooked homesteaders (7)

14 Mail in beer for missionary (7)

15 Rainbows are almost ghostly (7)

16 Finds cola shaken, set back (7)

19 Slipped away insanely pleased (7)

21 Stinking, so I'm one mess (7)

22 Birds' nests in Belgravia ryegrass (6)

24 Orchestra on railway From Moscow to Vladivostok? (5–7)

25 One Roman emperor is inside (4)

26 Presses plants, and hops after wobbly sprint (5,5)

DOWN

1 Seizes luggage (4)

2 Herb Regan has nothing on— nothing! (7)

3 Walk passed by Supreme Court? (14)

4 Confused a Zen aid, still confused (2,1,4)

5 Anoint oneself including chants (7)

7 Hair braided up, that's sweet (7)

8 Zany tends swans— that'll sell papers! (10)

9 Bad-tempered inspectors are ones who question witnesses (14)

13 Fish between two firearms—it's an old weapon (7,3)

17 See, I hear Tex or John—and a varmint (7)

18 If this poet followed Di, vending machine would appear (7)

19 No, I save the wrong way for avoidance (7)

20 So price slashed for Pacino film (7)

23 Dollar bills in a two-tone satchel (4)

CRYPTIC

CROSSWORD PUZZLE NUMBER SIX

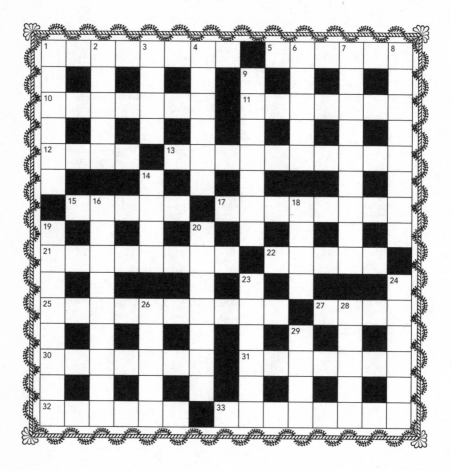

CROSS

1 Old man in trouble, with strings attached! (8)

5 Her zit treated, strings along! (6)

10 Men rant wildly, leaving just a trace (7)

11 Ripe as a decayed flowering shrub (7)

12 Jones and 500 follow this (4)

13 Overcomes disgruntled narcs' dents (10)

15 Retro paid leaves disappear—so stick it! (5)

17 Crones at odds with forefather (8)

21 A bag, a rut, awry, a root (8)

22 Horns have crust (5)

25 Eccentric, so super pro is doing well (10)

27 Wild animals ready to proceed (4)

30 Advances in highways (7)

31 Leader I treasure embraces nation (7)

32 Is it a rug, ragged and stringy as it is? (6)

33 One of the Marx Brothers almost follows car—with strings that are buttoned (8)

DOWN

1 Violently arming provides edge (6)

2 Mad? No, wanderer mistaken (5)

3 Track in President's office (4)

4 Buries, rest in pieces (6)

6 In toil I ached down to the bone! (5)

7 Do these an other way—they're prefixed to the main text (9)

8 Say again, right—fool in tree climbs up (8)

9 Inane is inane, inane (7)

14 Small dietary item is found back in some of the bric-a-brac (4)

16 I pour port, spilling it and making a collection (9)

18 Ineffective cure for tan (4)

19 Grasping and holding interest (8)

20 Attack and tear up grass, e.g. (7)

23 Some kind of dresser, Beau gets around old city (6)

24 Overhaul gun and small electronic device (6)

26 Five quit Pravda—that's the fashion (5)

28 Busy artery snarled pro rata without P.R. (5)

29 Josip Broz Jackson? (4)

CHAPTER TWELVE

RAGBAG

**Euphemisms, Highly Irregular Conjugations,
Tongue-Twisters, Theater-by-the Numbers,
Rhyming Slang, and Name Games**

*What's in a name? That which we call a rose
By any other name would smell as sweet.*

—William Shakespeare, *Romeo and Juliet*

Is the food tastier in a bistro than in a diner? Will a veterinarian take better care of your prize stallion than a horse doctor will? Would you prefer to travel on a rapid-transit coach or a subway car? These are questions that coiners of euphemisms confidently answer for us.

Euphemism, from the Greek *euphemismos* ("to speak well, or use words of good omen") is the substitution of a more agreeable word or phrase for one that is harsh, vulgar, unpleasant, or simply devalued by overuse. Euphemisms pop up most frequently to describe such things as death and disease, sexual and excretory functions, menial occupations, and all those things that we don't discriminate against: race, creed, color, age, national origin, and sexual orientation. But no honest, hardworking, unpretentious word is exempt from the euphemist's attempt to smarten it up a bit.

Tired of being a publicist? No problem—just reprint your business card and become a communications director. Don't want a used car? For the same price you can get one that's pre-owned. And if you don't crave a ground-meat patty for dinner, just order Salisbury steak.

The Greeks, as they usually are, were the first to engage in the practice of euphemism, and a notable example can be found in those disagreeable avenging divinities Megaera, Tsiphone, and Alecto, or as you probably know them, the Furies. They were usually depicted with snakes in their hair, which is the first clue that you might not want to invite them over for tea. The meaning of the three names pretty well cinches it: "jealousy," "blood vengeance," and "relentless pursuit." In Greek, the Furies are the *Erinyes*, but the wily old Greeks decided that it would be smarter to call them something nicer, in the hope that they would practice their mayhem elsewhere. In a verbal leap equivalent to rechristening Hitler as Mother Teresa, the Furies became known not as *Erinyes*, but as *Eumenides*, which means "the kindly ones." Aeschylus memorialized them in his play of that name.

The above calls to mind an old joke, which really belongs in another chapter, if anywhere, but such paltry details do not deter your author. A professor of Greek took his torn trousers to a Greek tailor, who asked him, "Euripides?" "Yes," said the professor, "Eumenides?"

The trappings of death have undergone constant change throughout history in an attempt to ameliorate the harshness of the reality. Where people once died, then expired, they later began to pass away (or pass on, pass over, or sometimes just pass), go to a better place, breathe their last, join their ancestors, find peace, cross over, reach the other side, meet their maker, be translated, give up the ghost, move to another world, be called to a higher service, receive their final reward, enter into eternal rest, or simply go home. From the fourteenth century, the dead body was known as a corpse, which gave it a nice Latinate softening; but when corpse became an unpleasant term, it was supplanted by shroud of clay, the remains, the deceased, the late so-and-so, the dear departed, the loved one, or, in the parlance of undertakers, the client.

Undertakers (originally people who did odd jobs) are no longer what they once were: gravediggers. But they're not undertakers any more, either; they have morphed to morticians, funeral directors, grief therapists, or arrangement counselors. The churchyards in which the bodies were buried, of course, are no longer usually churchyards, but they're not cemeteries or burial grounds, either. They are memorial parks, eternal resting places, peaceful valleys, or gardens of perpetual care. The box for the dead body became a coffin, a sarcophagus, a bier, a pall, and then a casket. Before too long that casket is bound to be known as a horizontal armoire.

People whose job requires them to deal with dirt and trash have also been upwardly mobile, at least in nomenclature. The British dustman and the American garbageman are relics of the past, having been supplanted by rubbish removers, trash collectors, refuse transporters, disposal specialists, sanitation engineers, and solid waste management technicians. Their colleagues, the janitors, find their jobs have been taken by porters, custodians, maintenance engineers, and building supervisors. And the charwoman or housemaid was transformed to a cleaning lady, a domestic, and then a housekeeper.

And if you're looking for an endless stream of appellations, try the oldest profession, whose members certainly aren't going to settle for being whores or even prostitutes or harlots, but from time to time have seemed to be as happy as hookers, chippies, strumpets, streetwalkers, call girls, business girls, courtesans, demimondaines, ladies of the evening, escorts, masseuses, or models. What the real models and masseuses are to call themselves is anybody's guess.

— ◆ —

People get touchy about all sorts of things. They'd rather not use a toilet or even a lovely euphemistic water closet, but might settle for a lavatory (not necessarily for hand-washing), a bathroom (not for taking a bath), a restroom (certainly not for taking a nap), a comfort station, a powder room, a public convenience, or a ladies' or gentlemen's lounge.

Those who used to be lame later became crippled, handicapped, disabled, physically challenged, and now differently abled. The only lame things now are excuses, and only golfers are handicapped. Old people became aged, then elderly, then senior citizens, retirees, seniors, pensioners (in Great Britain), and then golden agers. From there, it would seem there is no place to go, but the indefatigable euphemists are certain to find something more seemly than coot, codger, geezer, blue-hair, or old-timer to refer to the increasing numbers of octogenarians, nonagenarians, and centenarians.

There are infinite euphemisms to alter unfavorable perceptions of racial and ethnic groups, religious sectarians, military operations, and even such harmless physical phenomena as the dead-end street, which evolved to no exit, no outlet, blind alley, and then to the oh-so-elegant cul de sac. Anatomical parts and sexual practices are a hotbed, so to speak, of euphemism, but you've been able to dally with ample prurience in erotica elsewhere in this volume. In the interest of keeping the art of euphemism alive, your humble pen-pusher—that is, your author—offers the following coinages in the hope that they will soon become current throughout the land:

> Ditchdigger: *Earthwork Engineer*
> Busboy: *Food Equipment Relocator*
> Restroom attendant: *Evacuation Technician*
> Hospital patient: *Wellness Candidate*
> Dust: *Accumulated Ambient Resurfacing Material*
> Plane crash: *Aeronautical Progress Interruption*
> Cockroach: *Entomological Evolutionary Success*
> Pothole: *Split-Level Roadway Surface*
> Failing school grade: *Extraordinary Academic Evaluation*
> Salary cut: *Occupational Compensation Reallocation*
> Gambling loss: *Recreational Activities Funding Reapportion-ment*
> Stupid person: *Reverse Intelligence Expert*
> Immoral person: *Ethical Innovator*
> Criminal: *Legal Reinterpreter*
> Cobwebs: *Arachnoid Filigree*

—•◆•—

In a similar vein, trying to make things sound better (or worse) than they are, the philosopher Bertrand Russell, of all people, long, long ago, way back in the 1940s, invented a game of "conjugations" of "irregular verbs." It's more easily understood by citing Russell's famous example than by trying to explain it: "I am firm; you are obstinate; he is a pig-headed fool."

In 1948 a British publication, *The New Statesman and Nation*, sponsored a conjugation competition, and some of the winners included:

* I am sparkling; you are unusually talkative; he is drunk.
* I have the New Look; you have let down your hem; she has had that dress since 1934.
* I am beautiful; you have quite good features; she isn't bad-looking, if you like that type.
* I have reconsidered it; you have changed your mind; he has gone back on his word.

Now, for your conjugal pleasure—er, make that conjugational—here are a few irregular inflections dreamed up by your very own author:

* I am a person of faith; you are strict in your beliefs; he is a religious fanatic.
* I have impeccable taste; you are finicky; he is impossible to please.
* I am an astute money manager; you are a bit conservative; he is a tightwad.
* I am generous; you are careless with money; he spends like a drunken sailor.
* I pay my bills on a fixed schedule; you take your time settling up; he is a deadbeat.
* I try to stay fit; you are overly concerned about your physical well-being; he is a health nut.
* I enjoy a glass of wine or two; you sometimes overindulge; he is a sot.

* I love good food; you will eat anything; he has both feet in the trough.
* I am a trendy dresser; you tend to overdo it, dear; she looks like a ten-dollar whore.
* I appreciate fine things; you are a bit worldly; she is a grasping gold digger.
* I don't clutter my mind with irrelevancies; you're becoming forgetful; he has the memory of a flea.
* I don't want to look anorexic; you've put on a pound or two, haven't you?; she is a fat pig.
* I misspoke myself; you stretched the truth a wee bit; he lied through his teeth.
* I look at both sides of the question; you are indecisive; he flip-flops all over the place.
* I have the courage of my convictions; you are a bit inflexible; he has a closed mind.

—•—

Now, it's your turn, honored reader, to go to work because the next subject is tongue-twisters, and to get the full benefit, you've got to say them all aloud. As we all know, tongue-twisters are phrases that are deemed difficult to say, especially when repeated rapidly several times, usually because of the need to alternate between sets of similar but slightly different consonants, such as "She sells sea shells, etc." They are often used by elocution instructors to improve their students' enunciation, and at one time were a standard feature of auditions for radio announcers. Probably the most universally known tongue-twister, although in truth not really very difficult to say, is:

Peter Piper picked a peck of pickled peppers.
A peck of pickled peppers Peter Piper picked.

If Peter Piper picked a peck of pickled peppers,
Where's the peck of pickled peppers Peter Piper picked?

Mere child's play. *Guinness World Records* purports that the most difficult tongue-twister in English is "The sixth sick sheik's sixth sheep's
sick." Its status was so determined by one Ken Parkin of Teesside,
England, the author of *Anthology of British Tongue Twisters*. Another
candidate for most difficult is "The seething sea ceaseth and thus the
seething sea sufficeth us." This one is offered by William Poundstone, author of the intriguingly titled *Big Secrets: The Uncensored
Truth About All Sorts of Stuff You Are Never Supposed to Know.*

——•◆•——

Your sometimes tongue-tied author has come up with these
originals, which he finds hard enough to say under normal conditions,
let alone after a few samples of the dark beverage with the creamy
head made by the original publishers of *Guinness World Records.*

* Tina Turner, Twyla Tharp, and Tommy Tune were terribly
  troubled trying tirelessly to trim ten tinseled thistle trees for
  Tiny Tim.
* Susie Shaw's Chinese chauffeur Charlene says she saw Sam
  Shepard show ship-shape see-saws to Sans Souci's sushi
  sous-chef.
* Hey, bub, do gabby goggled gobs garbed in rubber garbage
  bags bug you?
* Bats might bite gnats by night, but note gnats might not bite
  nits or mites.
* Snippy cops with sippy cups and cheery chaps in snappy
  caps sip soup and chew cheesy chips in sloppy chop shops.
* Zsa Zsa, is this Sir Sacheverell Sitwell's sick sister Edith's
  sixth zither?

A British favorite of the author's concerns a woman who encounters a tinker working on pots and pans. She asks: "Are you copper-bottoming 'em, my man?" He replies: "No, 'm, I'm aluminiuming 'em, Mum." Note that *aluminium* is spelled and pronounced in the British way in five syllables, the accent on "min." Curiously, the tongue-twister becomes even more difficult if *aluminum* is given the American four-syllable pronunciation, accenting "lu."

Here now in no particular order of difficulty are some other notable tongue-twisters of the past. If you can do all of these three times without a flub, well, you probably need to relax more.

* Six sick hicks nick six slick bricks with picks and sticks.
* Peggy Babcock (you must say this one five times)
* Six thick thistle sticks. Six thick thistles stick.
* I slit the sheet, the sheet I slit, and on the slitted sheet I sit.
* Miss Sissy Smith's Fish Sauce Shop.
* Which witch wished which wicked wish?

Another kind of exercise is more of a straight pronunciation test. In *I Looked and I Listened* author Ben Gross reports that the following was used as part of an announcer's test at NBC radio (when there was an NBC radio):

"Penelope Cholmondely raised her azure eyes from the crabbed scenario. She meandered in the congeries of her memoirs. There was Algernon, a choleric artificer of icons and triptychs, who wanted to write a trilogy. For years she had stifled her risibilities with dour moods. His asthma caused him to sough like the zephyrs among the tamarack. He insisted upon being the cynosure even after a virulent attack of alopecia areata left him egregiously glabrous . . ."

—•—

Willard R. Espy in his *Almanac of Words at Play* provides this audition piece for would-be announcers at New York City's classical music station WQXR-FM:

"The old man with the flaccid face and dour expression grimaced when asked if he were conversant with zoology, mineralogy, or the culinary arts. 'Not to be secretive,' he said, 'I may tell you that I'd given precedence to the study of genealogy. But, since my father's demise, it has been my vagary to remain incognito because of an inexplicable, lamentable, and irreparable family schism. It resulted from a heinous crime, committed at our domicile by an impious scoundrel. To err is human . . . but his affair was so grievous that only my inherent acumen and consummate tact saved me.'"

—•—

There are some trick words in these tests. For example, Webster at one time insisted that *secretive* be pronounced with the accent on the second syllable, although most people preferred to accent the first syllable, and in later editions, that pronunciation has won out. *Precedence* used to be pronounced with the accent on the first syllable, but now the second syllable is permitted by most dictionaries. *Demise, vagary, lamentable, inexplicable, incognito, impious, acumen,* and even little *err* are words whose one-time preferred pronunciations differed from the way most people actually said them. The evolution of language and today's permissive dictionaries, however, have made such announcers' tests virtually obsolete. Notwithstanding this sad fact, your author has busied himself to come up with his own obsolete announcer's test in a totally baffling narrative. Even though nowadays you can say the words any way you like, some of them may at least give you pause:

—•◆•—

In the halcyon days of internecine tergiversation, a concupiscent chargé d'affaires at the Tanzanian consulate had the onerous assignment of arranging assignations amongst Zbigniew Brzezinski, Valery Giscard d'Estaing, Deng Xiao Peng, Angela Merkel, and Dmitri Medvedev.

"What a concatenation of blackguards," expatiated this amanuensis, who was a bona fide dilettante. "It's a veritable farrago of inextricable idiosyncrasies. They will discuss laissez-faire, hypotenuses, synapses, kamikazes, Clio, Melpomene, Mnemosyne, and other such viragoes, before arriving, apocalyptically, at the dénouement. A priori, it is de rigueur that I not err, though embarrassed and harassed vituperatively by such vagaries."

Grasping his shillelagh ribaldly, as though he were a mischievous member of Sinn Fein, he peregrinated, redolent with desuetude, to the environs of the soigné maitre d'.

"I speak not in synecdoche, hyperbole, hendiadys, litotes, or even metonymy," he descanted, "when I say the menu is to be table d'hôte—prix fixe. We'll start with a mélange of exquisite hors-d'oeuvres such as paté de foie gras, abalone, escargots, prosciutto, salmon mousse, macadamia and pistachio nuts, followed by tournedos in béchamel sauce, or maybe sauerbraten with endive, kohlrabi, and cilantro; then a nice Brie or Camembert with a demitasse of espresso or cappuccino, followed by a mere soupçon of Calvados, Cointreau, or Chartreuse."

"Are you desirous of proffering homage to Escoffier," asked the supercilious garçon, "or merely of producing a satiety?"

In this hiatus, the diplomatist, a quite pliant affiant, became exquisitely quiescent and riant, in order to assuage the boniface's irascibility.

"The artistes who will furnish vaudevillian divertissement," he specified, "will include a miscellany of eidolons of lauded divas, *primi ballerini assoluti*, *danseurs nobles*, ingenues, tragedians, and other virtuosi, of the magnitude of Amelita Galli-Curci, Eleanora Duse, Ignacy Jan Paderewski, Erwin Piscator, Eugène Ysaÿe, Josef Szigeti, Ernest Cecchetti, Jussi Björling, Eugène Goossens (fils), Beniamino Gigli, Feodor Ivanovitch Chaliapin, Vaslav Nijinsky, Frances Yeend, Olga Preobrajenska, Maya Pliesetskaya, and Olga Spessivtzeva.

"For the locale," he continued in his inimitable fashion, clandestinely flicking a gnat from a piece of gnocchi on his grosgrain habiliment, "I am contemplating a granary in Aberystwyth or Abergavenny or maybe Clywd (should we wish to be in Cymru), or perhaps Cannes or Caen, or Ixtapa or Oaxaca, or possibly even Mexia or Refugio."

"How about Gruene?"

"Ersatz—and indubitably despicable."

"Or Boerne?"

"No, too fin-de-siècle," grimaced the porcine legate with authoritative panache, concluding the desultory tête-à-tête.

Another type of announcer's test was related by Jerry Lewis on Larry King's television program. Lewis said he learned it from Johnny Carson's sidekick, Ed McMahon. It involves not only tricky pronunciation, but also the memorization and repetition of prodigiously complicated lists. The version mentioned by Lewis as having been used by NBC required the applicant to listen to another person recite, one at a time, a string of numbered items and then repeat them cumulatively, à la "The Twelve Days of Christmas." Here's how it goes:

"One hen; two ducks; three squawking geese; four Limerick oysters; five corpulent porpoises; six pairs of Don Alverso's patented tweezers; seven thousand Macedonian warriors in full battle array; eight brass monkeys from the ancient, sacred, secret crypts of Egypt; nine apathetic, sympathetic, diabetic old men on roller skates with a marked propensity toward procrastination and sloth; ten lyrical, spherical, empirical, and diabolical denizens of the deep who all stall around the corner of the quo of the quay of the quivery, all at the same time."

An alternate version of the last item in the list mentions "ten iridescent, effervescent, adolescent, convalescent wombats from the local chapter of the United Daughters of the Confederacy."

Many variations on this memory and pronunciation test abound, including this one often used around children's campfires when the ghost stories have finally palled:

"One fat hen; a couple of ducks; three baby brown bears; four rabbit-running hares; five fat, fidgety felines; six Simple Simons selling salt in Siam; seven slimy sailors sipping slop by the sea; eight elongated elephants escalating on an escalator; nine nasty-nosed nibbly-O's nibbling on the noses of nine nasty-nosed nibbly-I's; ten two-tone ten-ton transcontinental tanker trucks with tandem trailers, traveling from Tyler, Texas, to Tallahassee, Tennessee, trucking twelve tanks of Texaco true-test with Techroline on twenty-two tires with terrible treads."

Whew!

If you'd like to tease your brain now and give your tongue a rest, try the following puzzle. You've heard of painting by the numbers; well, this game might be called "Theater-by-the-Numbers." The object is to fill in the missing words in the title of a play or musical that also contains a number. In order to give you a fair shot at a perfect score so that you can brag to your friends, the names of the authors of the work are in parentheses following the numbers and the initials of the missing words. And if you're really stumped, the solutions follow. Go ahead and try. What have you got to lose, except your self-esteem?

1 T of V (Perelman, Nash, Weill)

2 G of V (Shakespeare)

3 M on a H (Abbott, Holm)

4 S in 3 A (Stein, Thomson)

5 F E (Shaffer)

6 C in S of an A (Pirandello)

7 K to B (Cohan)

D at 8 (Kaufman, Ferber)

10 L I (Christie)

12 A M (Rose)

The N of J 16 (Rand)

27 W of C (Williams)

The 39 S (Barlow, Buchan)

40 C (Allen, Grédy, Barillet)

42nd S (Stewart, Bramble, Warren, Dubin)

45 M to B (Cohan)

70, G, 70 (Ebb, Martin, Masteroff, Kander)

84 C C R (Hanff)

110 in the S (Nash, Jones, Schmidt)

1,000 C (Gardner)

50,000,000 F (Fields, Porter)

And may we have the envelope, please? The answers are: *One Touch of Venus, Two Gentlemen of Verona, Three Men on a Horse, Four Saints in Three Acts, Five Finger Exercise, Six Characters in Search of an Author, Seven Keys to Baldpate, Dinner at Eight, Ten Little Indians, Twelve Angry Men, The Night of January 16, Twenty-Seven Wagonloads of Cotton, The 39 Steps, Forty Carats, 42nd Street, Forty-five Minutes to Broadway, 70, Girls, 70, 84 Charing Cross Road, 110 in the Shade, A Thousand Clowns,* and *Fifty Million Frenchmen.* Now, quick, what's the total of all the numbers above? (Only kidding.)

Would you Adam and Eve it? It's time to rest your plates of meat, take off your tit for tat, and use your loaf of bread. The foregoing strangely expressed sentiment can be interpreted to mean: "Would you believe it? It's time to rest your feet, take off your hat, and use your head." The dialect used is cockney rhyming slang, which provides some extravagant examples of words gone wild.

A cockney by tradition is a Londoner born within the sound of Bow Bells, which are the church bells of St. Mary-le-Bow, Cheapside, in London's East End. More broadly, any working-class Londoner is referred to as a cockney. The term originated in the fourteenth century, according to *The Oxford Companion to English Language,* when "cokeneyes" were referred to in the poem "Piers Plowman." The word meant misshapen eggs that were fancifully supposed to have been laid by a cock instead of a hen; a cockeneye thus became a person who was an "odd egg." By 1368 Chaucer in *The Canterbury Tales* used the term "cokenay" to mean a simpleton or a fool. In the sixteenth century "cockney" was used derisively to mean a working-class person brought up in a city without any knowledge of real, i.e. country, life.

Well, that's one possibility. Another pundit speculates that the term "cockney" stemmed from the Norman French nickname for London: *le pais de cocaigne,* or the "Land of Cockayne"—a medieval concept that meant a place of hedonistic luxury. The French word *cocaigne* originally meant a small sugar cake typically sold at fairs. The name of the cake later symbolized all kinds of ease and pleasure. Today, of course, the land of hedonistic luxury would probably be regarded not as London, but as Hollywood, California, and "cockayne" would be spelled slightly differently.

However the term "cockney" originated, by the seventeenth century the notion of Bow Bells, limiting cockney-land to the East End of London, had entered the lore.

Rhyming slang was probably created sometime in the seventeenth century, first by criminals or entertainers—who were often one and the same, of course—to keep their communication secret from laypeople. The object being discussed was replaced by a word that rhymed with it ("meat" for "feet"), to which was prefixed another term ("plates of") to add to the confusion for the uninitiated. As spoken today, the second, rhyming word is usually dropped, so that only the first, nonrhyming term is used: "plates" meaning feet, "titfer" (instead of "tit for tat") for hat, and "loaf" (instead of "loaf of bread") for head. Other common slang includes "trouble and strife" (almost always shortened to "trouble," meaning wife), "apples and pears" (stairs), and "Hampstead Heath" (teeth).

Many of the terms for which the rhyming slang is used are vulgar, and the slang words provide a socially acceptable way to say them: "Brahms and Liszt" for pissed, "threepenny bits" for tits, "raspberry tart" for fart. If you think very creatively, you can probably devise for yourself the meanings of "William Pitt," "Bristol cities," "Blackpool rock," and "Berkshire hunt." A comprehensive dictionary can be found at cockneyrhymingslang.co.uk.

Please remember that you were warned in the title of this chapter that it's a ragbag, and in keeping with its hodge-podge status, it ends with a game that first came to your author's attention from musicians who played it in orchestra pits during longueurs in the score. What the conductor did during these periods was not reported. The object of the game is to provide a punning definition for the name of a famous composer, more than likely a foreign one. For example: "pub chatter" might suggest Bartok. Or try another: "Subject a college official to ennui" would be Borodin. Now that you have the hang of it, here are a few definitions; the answers, if they can really be called that, will be found at the end of this ragbag. Please let your punditry run wild.

* What to tell a tired hog
* The majority of the paintings
* Skillet to put on display
* Frequently astern
* Type of telephone signal
* That bank draft over there
* What to do after you aim
* Become increasingly elf-like
* Where to read about a legendary hero
* What to do when a soup bowl is thrown at you
* Hut where marriages are dissolved
* "Your problem this time?"
* Only the associate sorceress
* Put soft material on a jagged piece of winter sports equipment
* In favor of caffeinated beverages under unspecified conditions
* Whole bottle isn't necessary

As you can see, the game is best played with a fairly large pool of easily recognizable foreign names that lend themselves to fanciful punning. Artists are another category that suits this kind of foolery.

* Legal tender
* A large number
* In a bridge game, to fail to win a trick consisting only of deuces and treys
* German highway
* Only a fruit preserve
* Rang the woman on the phone
* The food table is this way
* Keep it to yourself
* Passenger vehicle to depart
* Irate
* The guy from Manila talks too much
* Armani, yes, but . . .
* Bird battle
* Sincere
* You—string player
* You—three musicians
* The final buss
* This annelid
* Anything happening?

And to leave you in a thoughtful mood, let's do it with philosophers.

* Wagon for use from morning to night
* Hello, laborer with a shovel!
* Is unable
* Objective pronoun
* Smash a sentry with your toe
* Not ath tight
* Kris Kringle's over there

* Time for the mall to open
* Recess in the wall
* Dad's girlfriend
* The Blessed Virgin has been in the sun

And now, ta-da, the answers! Composers—Respighi, Mozart, Chopin, Offenbach, Bizet, Janácek, Falla, Grofé, Hindemith, Khachaturian, Dvorák, Smetana, Shostakovich, Paderewski, Prokofiev, Glazunov. Artists—Monet, Manet, Toulouse-Lautrec, Audubon, Botticelli, Calder, Dubuffet, Donatello, van Gogh, Ingres, Filippino Lippi, Noguchi, Renoir, Ernst, Uccello, Utrillo, Velázquez, Vermeer, Watteau. Philosophers—Descartes, Heidegger, Kant, Hume, Kierkegaard, Luther, Santayana, Schopenhauer, Nietzsche, Pascal, Maritain.

L'ENVOI

"Wit has truth in it; wise cracking is simply calisthenics with words."
—Dorothy Parker

For years, your author has seen the term *L'Envoi*—or its English version, the plainspoken, no-nonsense *Envoy*—over paragraphs appended to various pieces of writing, without knowing exactly what it meant. As Webster's would have it, *L'Envoi*, from the French *envoyer* ("to send") is "a postscript, usually explanatory or commendatory, to a poem, essay, or book; specifically, a short fixed stanza pointing the moral, addressing some person, etc." This particular *envoi* will deal primarily with "etc."

Among the words gone wild encountered in the preparation of this volume, the wildest of all were those that Microsoft Word's spelling and grammar checker tried to thrust upon the text. This supposedly omniscient literary software, ostensibly intended to correct errors in spelling and usage made by ignorant literati, is a dangerous tool for a writer. In the first place, it can lull one into a sense of complacency by blithely accepting "no" when "know" is intended, or "accept" instead of "except," or even allowing you to write "butt" when you mean "but"—butt try to use a sentence with more than, say, fifteen words (like this one) and you get a stern reprimand that it's much too long. And even saying "it's too long" is likely to get you into trouble, as the officious spell-checker will strongly suggest that you probably mean *its*, even in instances when *it's* is correct.

This self-appointed arbiter of usage is emphatically fussy, often wrongly, about word choices—and anytime you use *whom*, it's ten-to-one it will insist you really mean *who*, even if *whom* is perfectly correct. It actually thinks Hemingway's *For Whom the Bell Tolls* should be *For Which the Bell Tolls*. On the other hand, write "To who it may concern," and the prissy grammar-checker passes it by without so much as a raised eyebrow. But whatever you do, try to avoid using *their*, *there*, and *they're* at all costs, or you'll send the poor electronic invigilator flailing in all directions in a tizzy of corrective action.

Microsoft's uncompromising checker has no truck with proper names, unless they're something common like John and Mary. Heaven forbid you wish to write about someone named Dagmar, who Microsoft insists should be Diagram, or Stanislas, who, if you let down your guard for a split second, will be rechristened Stainless. The noted actresses Sarah Siddons and Lillie Langtry are actually surnamed Saddens and Lengthy, if Microsoft has its facts straight. The checker earnestly believes that Sherlock Holmes would be much more appropriately named Cherokee Holmes. And, if for some outlandish reason, you wish to write of those Four Musketeers—Aramis, Athos, Porthos, and D'Artagnan, be exceedingly vigilant, or the spell-checker will have you telling the tale of Aromas, Pathos, Portholes, and [No spelling suggestion].

The works of Shakespeare seem to be especially problematic for the Word wizard. The tragedy of the Moor, it thinks, would be more elegantly named *Ethel* than *Othello*, and it much prefers Sir John Flagstaff to Sir John Falstaff. Shakespeare's *Two Gentlemen* are believed to come from *Vernon*, rather than *Verona*. Shylock of *The Merchant of Venice* is only an alias; his real name is Shellac. And Constable Dogberry would be more aptly named Dogbert—which just goes to show that the wondrous spell-checker reads Dilbert in the comics. What's more, you can see all these dramatis personae in that historic London theater Dreary Lane, which is near the River Thermos.

A few other *noms de Microsoft* include the famed tennis player Roger Fedora, the sultry German Blue Angel Marlene Detroit, the hobbit-creator J. R. R. Toluene, U.S. President Woodwork Wilson, conductor Andre Privet, reclusive author J. D. Slander, actors Carol Brunette and Ingrid Bagman, Hungarian composer Bela Partook, and the obviously excited Dutch painter Vincent van Gosh. If you doubt any of this, you can look it all up in *Bracelet's Familiar Quotations*.

Perhaps, however, the Microsoft word elves do know *something*, after all; they demand that Supreme Court Justice Antonin Scalia be known as Antiunion Scalier.

Computers, bless their vicious little hearts, provide the ultimate opportunity for words to go truly wild. One example is a game called "Googlewhacking," a pastime created for idlers with no useful work to do. Googlewhacking is not necessarily as libidinous an activity as it sounds. The object of the game is to enter two words into Google's search box that will yield one—and only one—reference. There is even a so-called "official" Googlewhacking Web site at googlewhack.com (which denies any affiliation with the Google organization, implying that you could also Yahoowhack or Bingwhack if you preferred). At the Web site you will find the full rules of the game and an opportunity to post your successful "whacks." The rules prescribe that the words should be entered without being enclosed in quotation marks, so that they need not appear consecutively in the document that is found. Obviously, mere word lists don't count. Much more fun, in the view of some players, including this one, is to use quotation marks around the two words, ensuring that they will be found only in conjunction with each other.

A few of the author's recent Googlewhack successes, together with the context in which they were used, are:

"Ethiopian iceberg"

(from a blog at lordoftheringsguide.com) " . . . Well I managed to sit through Harry Potter's run in with hundreds of Giant Wolf Spiders. Maby I won't be scared. And maby I'm an *Ethiopian iceberg* inspector too."

"Lilliputian whisky"

(from a gift site at whiskyfun.com) " . . . I'm sure you'll 'need' this *Lilliputian whisky* distillery for Christmas, won't you? At £19.95, it's a cheap way of owning your own, dust-gathering distillery, even if made in China . . ."

"Estonian marimba"

(from a German Web site devoted to a memorable musician at www.wolfgang-pachla.de) "The *Estonian Marimba* virtuoso Wolfgang Pachla plays his instrument so rapidly that he really earns the virtuoso title"

"Hillbilly sudoku"

(from a blog at sudoku.com.su) "Oh oh . . . an insult to Southern intelligence, Jane . . . that might draw some fire from our *hillbilly sudoku* friends . . . oops, did I really say that?"

And, finally, the author's favorite (so far):

"Presbyterian sushi"

(from wargamer.com) " . . . And if the local preachers get their cassocks in a wad, just chuck 'em into the lagoon and remind them of the local shark population's fondness for *Presbyterian sushi*. . . . Tolerance and great morale would soon become the norm at this base."

Keep in mind, when playing this game, that results may change from day to day as Web pages are edited or added and removed from the Internet. A few years ago, for example, the phrase "hillbilly ballet" drew only one Google hit; when it was entered more recently there were fifteen. Ah, the march of civilization!

Another source of computer fun is one of the free translating services available online. Put an English phrase into a foreign language, then back into English—and see what emerges. The results will almost certainly show clearly what is meant by "lost in translation." Look what happens to something simple like the well-known children's rhyme:

> Mary had a little lamb.
> Its fleece was white as snow.
> And everywhere that Mary went
> The lamb was sure to go.

When translated first to Greek, then to Russian, back to English, to French, and finally back to English once again, it comes out this way:

> Mary had the small lamb,
> Its quilts was beautiful like snow,
> And this Mary went,
> The ewe-lamb everywhere was exactly suits him.

It's no wonder that delegates to the United Nations have trouble reaching unanimity on issues infinitely more complex than Mary's quilted little lamb.

As a final example of words gone wild beyond belief, consider the gibberish into which Lincoln's Gettysburg Address is rendered when translated by an online service from English to French to Italian to Dutch to Portuguese and then back into English. Don't know what you were smoking that day, but honest, Abe, this is what they claim you said!

It commemorates points and seven years our parents were produced there in this continent a new person, who in freedom, and devoted to the proposal was envisaged, that all the right men are created.

Now is us in a civil Great War engaged, thus envisaged and thus devoted, by much time. We are found in a large battle field of this war. We are devote part of this field saw, as the final place to rest for they which gave their lives here that this person could live. Completely it is adapted and adapted that us who this would have to make.

But in a larger direction, we can devote cannot devote cannot anybody holy known as with the ground. Men, life and deads wildly, which fought here, forgotten that it examines, or in this one nobody, or no candles where the people can distant above our poor capacity from; they devoted to add or it removes. The world little note, nor remembers per much time what we say here, but is possible this never it do not forget they made here. To live is, earlier, here with work not concluded for us crowned; they that one here already it fought; here this noble sophisticated manner. It is more advances some so that we are here devoted with the great task that with that of those deads, honoured for, remains, we take them with the largest devotion with this cause for this last measurement that full we decide devoted at here demons strongly that those do not exceed deads in this person, under the god, new the birth—and out of freedom it will be killed that the government of the people, by the people, for people, ground not perish.

—◆—

Words don't get any wilder than that. And now, dear reader, the end, alas, is near, and as the gardener said when asked why he was cutting grass with a pair of scissors: "That's all there is; there isn't any mower."

ANSWERS TO PUZZLES

BYRD WATCHING

O	P	A	L		P	E	T	A		S	H	A	H	S
P	A	L	O		A	V	I	D		L	A	L	A	W
E	A	S	E		T	O	L	E		A	W	A	R	E
C	R	O	W	E	S	N	E	S	T		K	I	T	E
			S	P	I	N	S		U	S	E	N	ET	
A	T	F		H	E	E		T	R	U	E			
N	U	R	S	E	S		L	E	A	P	Y	E	A	R
T	R	E	W	S		M	A	X		E	E	R	I	E
E	N	T	A	I	L	E	D		O	R	S	I	N	O
		N	A	I	L		A	R	M		C	T	S	
D	U	E	N	N	A		A	L	D	A	S			
I	T	A	S		R	O	B	B	I	N	S	E	G	G
V	I	G	O	R		L	O	I	N		G	R	O	W
E	L	E	N	A		E	D	N	A		T	I	N	E
S	E	R	G	E		G	E	O	L		S	E	E	N

CHANGING COURSES

	C	O	B	S		C	V	I	I		P	U	P	A
	O	W	E	N		R	A	M	S		A	N	I	S
	U	N	C	L	E	A	R	P	H	Y	S	I	C	S
C	L	E	O		I	B	N			A	S	C	O	T
A	I	R	M	E	N	B	I	O	L	O	G	Y		
O	S	S	I	E		E	S	P	Y		O	C	H	S
			N	R	C		H	A	R	P		L	E	O
F	R	A	G	I	L	E		L	I	S	T	E	N	S
R	O	D		E	A	C	H		C	A	R			
A	T	O	P		R	O	I	S		L	U	S	T	S
		P	E	N	A	L	G	E	O	M	E	T	R	Y
A	S	T	R	O			H	M	S		C	O	O	N
S	H	I	N	G	L	E	H	I	S	T	O	R	Y	
T	I	V	O		B	R	A	T		I	S	E	E	
A	P	E	D		J	E	T	E		L	T	D	S	

DISORDERLY CONDUCT

```
H E A R D . T R A D . D A R T
O L L I E . R E T E . A V E R
W I L D B E A S T S . D O N E
T O O . S T L O U I S . N E Y
O T T S . A E R . S R I . . .
. . U P S E T S T O M A C H
C O S B Y . S E E . M I L E
O L E S T R A . A D D E D O N
L A L O . E R A . D R A Y S
O F F I C E R S M E S S .
. L I L . U A L . E S S E
P A L . A S I N F U L . H E S
A L E E . O D D F E L L O W S
D O G S . F E E L . D O N E E
S T O P . F A R E . S T E R N
```

LETTER PERFECT

```
C A S A B A . . A N A L O G
A M O R A L . S E R E N E
V O W E L S . F A T A L I S T
E S S . O M A N I . I C E T
. R E P A C K . O S A T O
A N E A R . W E L L E S
B I K I N I . T E A R . E W E
U S E D . S M I T H . A R A N
T I S . O L E O . R O C O C O
. L E A D U P . P E S O S
A R M E D . I S L E T S .
B E A T . S A L O N . D D E
A D R O I T L Y . I N B O R N
S U N U N U . D E A R E R
E X I T E D . S Y Z Y G Y
```

MINDING PEAS AND CUES

S	N	A	P		C	O	P	E		S	W	I	S	S
E	U	R	O		U	V	E	A		T	E	N	E	T
A	D	E	S		R	E	A	R		R	E	T	R	O
S	E	A	S	P	A	N		E	Y	E	D	E	A	L
	E	A	T		A	D	I	T		L	I	E		
A	L	L		S	I	P	C		P	C	T			
B	E	A	M	O	V	I	E		H	O	S	T	S	
I	A	M	A		E	S	T	O	P		N	C	A	A
E	D	A	M	S		O	W	E	B	E	A	U	X	
	A	P	T		N	E	R	O		R	T	E		
R	A	H		O	I	S	E		F	R	A			
E	W	E	B	O	A	T		C	U	E	T	I	P	S
S	I	R	E	N		A	T	O	M		O	R	A	L
E	R	O	S	E		T	O	R	E		L	A	R	A
T	E	N	O	R		E	O	N	S		L	E	A	P

NO END IN SIGHT

A	S	I	A	N		M	A	P	S		S	L	A	B
D	O	N	H	O		I	C	E	T		T	A	R	A
U	N	F	I	N	I	S	H	E	D	S	Y	M	P	H
E	G	O		E	N	T	E	R		A	L	A	S	S
		H	E	I	R		E	T	U	I				
A	B	R	I	D	G	E	D	D	I	C	T	I	O	N
F	E	E	D		O	A	R		N	E	E	D	L	E
L	E	V		T	O	D				I	E	R		
A	C	U	R	S	E		M	I	O		B	O	U	V
T	H	E	E	N	D	L	E	S	S	S	U	M	M	E
	C	I	T	I		J	O	E	Y					
P	R	O	O	F		A	N	O	L	E		A	L	G
I	N	S	U	F	F	I	C	I	E	N	T	F	U	N
P	A	L	P		I	S	O	N		T	E	T	R	A
E	S	O	S		B	E	S	T		O	N	S	E	T

SURPRISE ENDINGS

¹Y	²O	³G	⁴A		⁵S	⁶A	⁷L	⁸A	⁹D		¹⁰A	¹¹P	¹²E	¹³D

Crossword grid — SURPRISE ENDINGS

Across/down answers shown in grid:

Row 1: Y O G A ■ S A L A D ■ A P E D
Row 2: S L A V ■ T O I L E ■ V I L E
Row 3: E D G A R A L L A N P O E M S
Row 4: R E S T O N ■ O N I O N ■ ■ ■
Row 5: ■ ■ A U D I ■ O E O ■ A L A
Row 6: G E O R G E S A N D P A P E R
Row 7: O A T ■ H E L M ■ S P E N T
Row 8: D R E D ■ S E A T S ■ O R N O
Row 9: O W L E T ■ T O E D ■ C I I
Row 10: W I L L I A M I N G E N U E S
Row 11: N G O ■ A R A ■ S M E E ■ ■
Row 12: ■ ■ G R I D S ■ E R A S E S
Row 13: T H O M A S M A N N E R I S M
Row 14: S A D E ■ E A T A T ■ E L M O
Row 15: E D E N ■ S N O B S ■ R O E G

WINNING WORDS

Crossword grid — WINNING WORDS

Row 1: M A L L ■ T R A U M A ■ S L R
Row 2: A R I A ■ A I R B A G ■ P O A
Row 3: S U C C E D A N E U M ■ O G G
Row 4: O B I T S ■ T E R M ■ A L O U
Row 5: N A T I O N A L ■ A E S I R
Row 6: ■ ■ C P I ■ H U S S A R S
Row 7: D I X ■ S C U B A ■ L A T H E
Row 8: I N A S ■ E R E C T ■ D O E R
Row 9: E T N A S ■ L E K O S ■ R A F
Row 10: S E T T E R S ■ B O A ■ ■
Row 11: ■ R H Y M E ■ S P E L L I N G
Row 12: I N O R ■ C U T E ■ A L G O L
Row 13: T I S ■ P O C O C U R A N T E
Row 14: A N I ■ C A L L A S ■ H I E S
Row 15: R G S ■ S T A I N S ■ S S S S

WORD PLACEMENT

T	A	M	E		B	A	S	H		E	S	T	E	R
I	T	E	S		E	T	T	A		V	I	O	L	A
T	H	E	C	O	L	L	A	R		E	E	R	I	E
H	O	T		M	I	A		D	E	N	S			
E	S	S	E	N	E	S		T	A	S	T	E	N	O
		B	I	S	T	R	O	S		A	V	E	R	
C	O	R	B	U		I	D	E		S	I	R	E	
O	N	A		M	A	L	C	O	L	M		T	O	O
A	T	T	S		T	A	C		U	M	A	S	S	
S	O	S	O		Q	U	I	B	B	L	E			
T	W	O	F	O	U	R		E	U	L	A	L	I	E
		T	R	E	E		R	N	A		E	N	D	
L	O	R	E	N		A	H	I	G	H	N	O	T	E
O	R	O	N	O		T	O	N	E		O	V	E	N
W	A	I	S	T		E	D	G	E		S	I	R	S

X-RATED

G	O	O	F		C	A	S	T	S		F	E	T	A
U	S	N	A		O	V	A	R	Y		O	L	I	N
S	T	Y	X		A	I	L	E	S		X	E	N	A
H	E	X	L	E	X	S	E	X	T	E	X	M	E	X
		A	X	I	O	M		E	L	O	I	S	E	
F	A	U	X	P	A	S		I	M	A	X			
M	U	S	S	E	L		X	L	S		C	O	R	A
A	R	E	A	L		A	X	L		R	O	P	E	R
M	A	R	K		P	B	X		M	A	X	E	N	E
		M	A	R	S		B	U	B	B	L	E	S	
P	L	E	A	S	E		M	A	M	B	O			
A	I	X	X	I	X	B	I	X	M	I	X		F	I	X
O	B	I	T		I	R	A	T	E		L	A	C	Y
L	E	L	A		E	A	T	E	R		O	R	E	L
I	L	E	X		S	C	A	R	S		X	E	R	O

ACROSTIC PUZZLE SOLUTIONS

NUMBER 1:

"But there are many tragedies in her family besides this affair of the curate. Her own sister, Mrs. Jekyll, had a most unhappy life through no fault of her own. I am sorry to say she was ultimately so broken-hearted that she went into a convent, or on to the operatic stage, I forget which."—Oscar Wilde, *An Ideal Husband*

A. Oh, What a Lovely War!
B. Speaker of the House
C. Catcher in the Rye
D. Arch of Triumph
E. Rube
F. Watch on the Rhine
G. Iambs
H. Loewe
I. Dotty
J. Entertainment Tonight!
K. Author! Author!
L. Noises Off
M. Iggy
N. Das Rheingold
O. Efforts
P. Attest
Q. Lawlessly
R. Hernia
S. Ursa Minor
T. Seiji
U. Biff
V. Attempt
W. Namesake
X. Dorothy Sayers

NUMBER 2:

"I have noticed through experience and through my own observations that Providence, Nature, God, or what I would call the Power of Creation seems to favor human beings who accept and love life unconditionally, and I am certainly one who does with all my heart."—Arthur Rubinstein, Poland

A. A Tale of Two Cities
B. Ruddigore
C. Tosca
D. High-hat
E. Ulanova
F. Royal Philharmonic Orchestra
G. Refined
H. Under the Yum Yum Tree
I. Bach
J. In vino veritas
K. Novelist
L. Sleeping Beauty
M. Two Gentlemen of Verona
N. Echo
O. Inched
P. Natch
Q. Powwow
R. Oxonian
S. Loch Lomond
T. Adapt
U. New World
V. Death

NUMBER 3:

"The great and central virtue of Shakespeare was not achieved by taking thought, for thought cannot create a world; it can only understand one when one has been created. Shakespeare, starting with the world no man has made and never indeed abandoning it, made many worlds within it."—Mark Van Doren, *Shakespeare*

- A. Mehta
- B. A Little Night Music
- C. Renata Scotto
- D. Kindergarten
- E. Vic
- F. Anne Hathaway
- G. No, No, Nanette
- H. Don't Drink the Water
- I. Ode to A Nightingale
- J. Right-hand man
- K. Echo Bay
- L. North and South
- M. Saw red
- N. Hubble
- O. A Streetcar Named Desire
- P. Kowtow
- Q. Ed Wynn
- R. Sarah Siddons
- S. Persephone
- T. Evade
- U. Acuff
- V. Review
- W. England

CRYPTIC CROSSWORD ANSWERS

CRYPTIC

PUZZLE ONE

1	2	3	4	5	6	7	8	9	10	11	12	13	14	15
S	T	A	T	U	E	O	F	L	I	B	E	R	T	Y
P	■	S	■	N	■	D	■	I	■	A	■	A	■	O
A	R	T	I	C	H	O	K	E	■	R	I	L	E	D
R	■	R	■	L	■	R	■	U	■	O	■	P	■	E
T	R	O	P	E	S	■	S	T	E	N	D	H	A	L
A	■	N	■	A	■	H	■	E	■	E	■	■	■	E
■	N	A	R	N	I	A	■	N	A	T	T	I	E	R
S	■	U	■	■	■	N	■	A	■	■	■	N	■	S
T	U	T	O	R	E	D	■	N	O	M	A	D	S	■
A	■	■	■	I	■	I	■	T	■	I	■	O	■	H
R	E	P	O	S	I	N	G	■	P	S	Y	C	H	E
T	■	R	■	O	■	G	■	I	■	S	■	H	■	D
R	A	I	T	T	■	O	U	T	L	I	V	I	N	G
E	■	M	■	T	■	F	■	C	■	N	■	N	■	E
K	E	E	P	O	F	F	T	H	E	G	R	A	S	S

EXPLANATIONS

ACROSS:

1 Anagram of STATE-BUILT FOYER

9 ART (paintings)-I-CHOKE (smother)

10 R(O)ILED ("O, no" = without O)

11 T(ROP)ES—PRO is rearranged; SET is reversed

12 Anagram of THE LANDS

14 Anagram of IRANIAN, less one I (eye)

15 NAT (King Cole) + TIER (row)

18 TUT (Egyptian king) + O (love, in tennis) + RED (Communist)

20 Anagram of DAMONS

23 R-EPOS-ING (RING=Wagnerian cycle, EPOS=heroic poem)

25 Two meanings

27 Homophones RAITT and rate

28 Anagram of VIOLIN GUT

29 Two meanings of phrase

DOWN:

1 Initial letters of Seems Particularly Astute Ruling The Area

2 ASTRONAUT = Sally Ride or rider in spaceship

3 UNCLE ANdy

4 goOD OR

5 LIEU (place) + TENANT (occupant)

6 BAR (saloon) + ONET (anagram of tone)

7 immoRAL PHotograph, with "Waldo" as an added hint

8 Anagram of YES, OLDER

13 HAN (Solo) + DINGO (Australian dog) + FF (very loud in music)

16 Anagram of IN OLD CHAIN, with L (left) out

17 START (begin) + RE (about) + K (a thousand)

19 Anagram of RIOTS TO

21 MISS + anagram of GIN

22 Two meanings

24 Two meanings

26 IT CHafes

CRYPTIC

PUZZLE TWO

	¹T		²O		³G		⁴D			⁵W		⁶C	
⁷P	O	R	C	E	L	A	I	N		⁸B	A	T	O	N
	T		E		A		S	⁹K		T		N	
¹⁰G	A	L	L	O	N		¹¹C	O	N	T	E	S	S	A
	L		O		C			O		R		E	
¹²O	I	N	T	M	E	¹³N	T	¹⁴C	O	L	O	R	S
	T					A		K		O		V	
¹⁵S	A	N	¹⁶F	R	¹⁷A	N	C	I	S	C	O	B	A	Y
	R		R		R		I					T	
¹⁸B	I	K	I	N	I		¹⁹T	²⁰O	R	²¹N	A	D	I	C
	A		G		S			E		V		O	
²²S	N	E	A	K	E	R	²³S	²⁴D	U	E	N	N	A
	I		T		N		H	A		N		I	
²⁵A	S	S	E	T		²⁶T	O	M	C	R	U	I	S	E
	M		S				P		T		E		T	

EXPLANATIONS

ACROSS:

7 POR-CELAI (anagram of Alice)-N

8 BATON (Rouge) = capital (of Louisiana)

10 GAL (miss) + LON (Chaney)

11 Anagram of CASES NOT

12 Anagram of TINT ON ME

14 Two meanings

15 Anagram of FANCY BASIC SONAR

18 ruBIK IN Ireland

19 TORN (ripped) + ADIC (anagram of acid)

22 SNE-AK (Alaska)-ERS

24 DUE + NNA (Ann reversed)

25 AS (like) + SET (television)

26 TOM (cat or turkey) + CRUISE (voyage)

DOWN:

1 Anagram of MILITIA START ON A

2 OCE (anagram of CEO) + LOT (vacant land)

3 G (thousand) + LANCE (spear)

4 hinDI SCribbling

5 LOO (john in England) positioned under WATER

6 Anagram of CONTRITION SAVES

9 KNOCKS sounds like Knox

13 TAC-I-T (I surrounded by TACT = diplomacy)

16 F-RIG-ATES (FATES = Greek goddesses, RIG = assemble)

17 HARI'S ENclave

20 RED (Communist) + ACT (measure)

21 A + VENUE (place)

23 Anagram of POSH

CRYPTIC

PUZZLE THREE

¹R	E	²D	³W	⁴H	I	T	⁵E	A	⁶N	D
I		I	O	O		M	O		E	

(Crossword grid)

Row 1: ¹R E ²D ³W ⁴H I T ⁵E A ⁶N D ■ ⁷B L U ⁸E
Row 2: I ■ I ■ O ■ O ■ M ■ O ■ E ■ B
Row 3: ⁹C O L O N ■ ¹⁰S K I M P ■ ¹¹A P E
Row 4: H ■ A ■ O ■ C ■ S ■ E ■ S ■ N
Row 5: ¹²A F T E R M A T H ■ ¹³S C E N E
Row 6: R ■ O ■ ■ N ■ T ■ T ■ S ■ Z
Row 7: ¹⁴D A R E ¹⁵D ■ ¹⁶I N ¹⁷C H E D ■ ■ E
Row 8: T ■ Y ■ O ■ N ■ O ■ R ■ ¹⁸I ■ R
Row 9: H ■ ■ ¹⁹O N E I L L ■ ²⁰S A N D S
Row 10: E ■ ²¹S ■ I ■ ■ L ■ ■ S ■ C
Row 11: ²²T O P A Z ■ ²³G O N D ²⁴O L I E R
Row 12: H ■ O ■ E ■ U ■ N ■ U ■ G ■ O
Row 13: ²⁵I N K ■ ²⁶T H E T A ■ ²⁷T A N G O
Row 14: R ■ E ■ T ■ S ■ D ■ R ■ I ■ G
Row 15: ²⁸D E N N I S T H E M E N A C E

EXPLANATIONS

ACROSS:

1 RED (Communist) + WHITE (colorless) + BLUE (sad)

9 COL (abbreviation of colonel) + ON

10 maSK IMPersonator

11 Anagram of PEA

12 AFTER (following) + MATH (arithmetic)

13 Homophones SCENE and seen

14 Anagram of DREAD

16 Anagram of CHIN + ED (editor abbreviated)

19 ONE + ILL

20 Two meanings

22 Initial letters of Turquoise, Opal, Pearl, Amethyst, Zircon

23 Anagram of LOG ON RIDE

25 (dr = doctor) INK

26 THE + TA (Cockney thanks)

27 Anagram of NO TAG

28 Anagram of MEAN SCENE HINTED

DOWN:

1 Anagram of HER CHART HID DIRT

2 Anagram of DAIRY LOT

3 IdaHO NORth

4 Anagram of IN TOSCA IN

5 IsIAM IS Holding

6 DO-PEST-ERS

7 Anagram of E-SALES

8 Anagram of ONCE GEEZER'S ROBE

15 Anagram of IT ZONED IT

17 Anagram of LONDON ACE

18 IN SIGN I Asked

21 Anagram of PENS O.K.

23 Homophones GUEST and guessed

24 Anagram of ROUTE

CRYPTIC

PUZZLE FOUR

¹E	L	²G	A	³R	■	⁴P	A	⁵S	D	⁶E	D	⁷E	U	⁸X
Q	■	O	■	H	■	R	■	A	■	N	■	X	■	Y
⁹U	K	U	L	E	L	E	■	¹⁰P	A	R	T	I	A	L
U	■	L	■	I	■	T	■	P	■	A	■	S	■	O
¹¹S	T	A	M	M	E	R	■	¹²H	I	G	H	T	O	P
■	■	S	■	S	■	¹³I	¹⁴T	O	■	E	■	■	■	H
¹⁵A	C	H	E	■	¹⁶B	A	R	■	■	¹⁷D	U	¹⁸M	B	O
R	■	E	■	■	¹⁹L	O	²⁰L	■	■	A	■	N	■	N
²¹T	O	S	C	²²A	■	■	²³P	A	N	■	²⁴O	G	L	E
I	■	■	■	I	■	²⁵S	E	T	■	²⁶S	■	N	■	■
²⁷E	M	²⁸B	A	R	G	O	■	²⁹T	O	P	P	I	N	³⁰G
S	■	A	■	C	■	D	■	I	■	A	■	F	■	R
³¹H	O	N	O	R	E	D	■	³²C	O	R	S	I	C	A
A	■	J	■	E	■	E	■	E	■	T	■	C	■	C
³³W	O	O	D	W	I	N	D	S	■	³⁴A	W	O	K	E

EXPLANATIONS

ACROSS:

1 Anagram of LAGER

4 Anagram of SEX PAD DUE

9 Two meanings of strings, with islands suggesting Hawaii

10 Anagram of A TRIP AL

11 STA-MME-R (RATS reversed, around MME = madame)

12 Anagram of HIP GOTH

13 IT Or

15 Anagram of EACH

16 Two meanings

17 memoranDUM BOring

19 LOL (it a)

21 Anagram of ASCOT

23 NAP is reversed

24 Anagram of LEGO

25 Two meanings

27 EM (ME reversed) + BAR + GO

29 Two meanings

31 Anagram of OH NO RED

32 Anagram of OSCAR around IC (I see)

33 WOOD (forest) + WINDS (breezes)

34 A WOK Easily

Down:

1 Anagram of QUEUES, less E (direction)

2 Anagram of GALOSHES with U (you)

3 Anagram of HEM SIR

4 Anagram of PERT LIAR

5 wineSAP PHObia

6 Anagram of ANGERED

7 EXI-S-T (S = south)

8 Anagram of PHONEY LOX

14 MeTRO PErsonnel

15 Anagram of I WEAR HATS

18 Anagram of IN MAGIC OF

20 L-ATTIC-ES (LES = the French)

22 (H)AIR CREW

25 SO (su)DDEN (without US)

26 SP-ART-A (SPA=resort)

28 Anagram of JOB AN

30 Two meanings

CRYPTIC

PUZZLE FIVE

1	2	3	4	5	6	7	8	9	10	11	12	13	14	15
¹B	O	²O	K	³C	R	⁴I	T	⁵I	C	█	⁶O	⁷D	I	⁸N
A	█	R	█	O	█	N	█	N	█	⁹C	█	E	█	E
¹⁰G	R	E	E	N	P	A	S	T	U	R	E	S	█	W
S	█	G	█	S	█	D	█	O	█	O	█	S	█	S
█	¹¹M	A	N	T	R	A	█	¹²N	E	S	T	E	R	S
¹³G	█	N	█	I	█	Z	█	E	█	S	█	R	█	T
¹⁴A	P	O	S	T	L	E	█	¹⁵S	P	E	C	T	R	A
T	█	█	█	U	█	█	█	█	█	X	█	█	█	N
¹⁶L	O	¹⁷C	A	T	E	¹⁸S	█	¹⁹E	L	A	P	²⁰S	E	D
I	█	R	█	I	█	P	█	V	█	M	█	E	█	S
²¹N	O	I	S	O	M	E	█	²²A	V	I	A	R	Y	█
G	█	T	█	N	█	N	█	S	█	N	█	P	█	²³O
G	█	²⁴T	R	A	N	S	S	I	B	E	R	I	A	N
U	█	E	█	L	█	E	█	O	█	R	█	C	█	E
²⁵N	E	R	O	█	²⁶P	R	I	N	T	S	H	O	P	S

EXPLANATIONS

ACROSS:

1 Anagram of CIO BRICK TO

6 Anagram of DINO

10 GREEN (ecologically correct) + PASTURES (grazing lands)

11 huMAN TRAgedy

12 Anagram of RESENTS

14 A-POST-LE (ALE = beer, POST = mail)

15 SPECTRA(L)

16 Anagram of COLA + SET reversed

19 Anagram of PLEASED

21 Anagram of SO I'M ONE

22 BelgrAVIA RYegrass

24 Two meanings

25 oNE ROman

26 Anagram of SPRINT + HOPS

DOWN:

1 Two meanings

2 O-REGAN-O

3 Two meanings

4 Anagram of A ZEN AID

5 anoINT ONESelf

7 TRESSED (braided), up (i.e., reversed)

8 Anagram of TENDS SWANS

9 Two meanings

13 GAT-LING-GUN (LING = fish, GAT, GUN = firearms)

17 C (see) + RITTER (Tex or John)

18 (DI)SPENSER

19 NO I SAVE (wrong way, i.e. reversed)

20 Anagram of SO PRICE

23 two-tONE-Satchel

CRYPTIC

PUZZLE SIX

1 M	A	2 N	D	3 O	L	4 I	N	■	5 Z	6 I	T	7 H	E	8 R
A	■	O	■	V	■	N	■	9 A	■	L	■	E	■	E
10 R	E	M	N	A	N	T	■	11 S	P	I	R	A	E	A
G	■	A	■	L	■	E	■	I	■	A	■	D	■	S
12 I	N	D	Y	■	13 T	R	A	N	S	C	E	N	D	S
N	■	■	■	14 C	■	S	■	I	■	■	■	O	■	E
■	15 S	16 P	E	A	R	■	17 A	N	C	18 E	S	T	O	R
19 G	■	O	■	R	■	20 A	■	E	■	C	■	E	■	T
21 R	U	T	A	B	A	G	A	■	22 B	R	A	S	S	■
I	■	P	■	■	■	G	■	23 B	■	U	■	■	■	24 R
25 P	R	O	S	26 P	E	R	O	U	S	■	27 G	28 A	M	E
P	■	U	■	R	■	E	■	R	■	29 T	■	O	■	V
30 I	N	R	O	A	D	S	■	31 E	R	I	T	R	E	A
N	■	R	■	D	■	S	■	A	■	T	■	T	■	M
32 G	U	I	T	A	R	■	33 A	U	T	O	H	A	R	P

EXPLANATIONS

ACROSS:

1 Anagram of OLD MAN IN

5 Anagram of HER ZIT

10 Anagram of MEN RANT

11 Anagram of RIPE AS A

12 Two meanings

13 Anagram of NARCS' DENTS

15 (DI)S(AP)PEAR (retro PAID, i.e. in reverse order, leaves, i.e. is removed from, "disappear")

17 Anagram of CRONES AT

21 Anagram of A BAG A RUT

22 Two meanings

25 Anagram of SO SUPER PRO

27 Two meanings

30 IN + ROADS (highways)

31 leadER I TREAsure

32 Anagram of IT A RUG

33 AUTO (car) + HARP(O) (one of the Marx Brothers almost)

DOWN:

1 Anagram of ARMING

2 Anagram of MAD NO

3 Two meanings

4 Anagram of REST IN

6 tolL I AChed

7 Anagram of DO THESE AN

8 R (right) + ASS (fool) in E-ERT (tree reversed)

9 Anagram of INANE IS

14 bric-a-BRAC (reversed)

16 Anagram of I POUR PORT

18 Anagram of CURE

19 Two meanings

20 Anagram of GRASS, E.G.

23 B-UR (old city)-EAU

24 REV (gun) + AMP (electronic device)

26 PRA(V)DA (V = 5)

28 Anagram of PRO RATA, without PR

29 Two meanings

INDEX